got milk?® the cookie book

got milk? the cookie book

by Peggy Cullen

Photographs by Rita Maas

CHRONICLE BOOKS

SAN FRANCISCO

For Andy and Raychel, who sweeten my life

Library of Congress Cataloging-in-Publication Data available.

ISBN 0-8118-2646-5

Printed in Hong Kong.

Food Stylist: Michael Pederson
Prop Stylists: Kemper Heyers and Cathy Cook
Photographer's Assistant: Matthew Kesterson
Book Design: Laura Lovett
Typeset in Hoffmann with Double Digits Round

Distributed in Canada by Raincoast Books
9050 Shaughnessy Street
Vancouver, British Columbia V6P 6E5

10 9 8 7 6 5 4 3 2 1

Chronicle Books LLC
85 Second Street
San Francisco, California 94105

www.chroniclebooks.com

Contents

Cookies and Me

If there's such a thing as a baking gene, I've got it—passed down on my mother's side from both her father and mother's families. Or perhaps my love of baking is cultural: the Eastern European women of my grandmother's generation filled their homes with the aromas of strudel, rugulah, and **kikheleh** (Yiddish for cookies).

My mother, an artist, instilled an affection for baking in my brother and me at a tender age. Our first project was to combine flour, salt, water, and food color into a batch of homemade play-dough. Mastering that, we moved on to more advanced activities, such as pressing raisin eyes into gingerbread men. Eventually we helped her make the dough, cut the shapes, and bake the cookies. By our pre-school standards these were grown-up and exciting endeavors.

Cookie baking is a wonderful way to introduce kids to the kitchen. In most cases it requires little skill beyond stirring and scooping. You needn't be an experienced baker to lead children through the process and turn out perfect cookies. Show them how to decorate cookies, and you bring the craft of cookie making into the realm of edible art. But you certainly don't have to have kids on hand to enjoy making and eating cookies. The waft of cookies baking in the oven makes a house (or apartment) feel cozy.

Cookie baking is a good place for wannabe bakers to start. Cake and pastry making usually require a number of elements (frostings, fillings, doughs, and batters) and more advanced techniques. Cookie making generally means mixing a simple dough and scooping, rolling, or piping it onto a baking sheet. You can learn all the basic skills by learning to bake cookies.

This book is written with the beginning baker in mind, but with recipes that appeal to the most experienced cookie eater. At the beginning of each section is general information and helpful tips that relate to those cookies. Read each section's introduction before you bake; it helps to demystify the cookie-making process. Knowledge breeds confidence. And that makes baking much more fun.

Milk and Cookies

Milk and cookies are a perfect pair. It's hard to put your finger on exactly why that's so. I've interviewed the experts. They have no explanation. I've questioned the kids. They say it's better than soda or juice—milk with cookies is simply the best.

The combination of cookies and milk is practically a cultural icon. Fed to us as children, craved as adults, cookies and milk, like peanut butter and jelly, are imbedded in our collective culinary consciousness.

When it comes to drinking milk with cookies there are dunkers, sippers, and guzzlers. The type of milk drinker you are is inspired by the kind of cookie you eat.

Crisp, dry cookies, such as gingersnaps and biscotti, can soak up a lot of milk and still maintain their form. Who can resist the urge to dunk? Whether dipping into a hot cappuccino or a cold glass of milk, you can drink a lot of latte off the end of your cookie.

Delicate dress-up cookies such as tuiles, lace, and meringues are nibbled demurely in polite company, at a dinner party or dessert buffet. You must remember to take small bites, chew with your mouth closed—and sip your milk.

Chocolate chip cookies, warm from the oven, are often eaten with wild abandon. The preferred way to drink milk with warm cookies is to stand in front of the open fridge and guzzle it straight from the carton.

Cookies are the ideal sweet for people on the go. They're hand-held, portable, and easy to eat. Kids like the fact that cookies don't require forks or plates. They're a welcome contribution to a classroom, meeting, or potluck party. The only thing that improves a cookie is a glass of milk.

From Cow to Carton

A cow can't give milk until it has given birth to a calf. It usually has its first calf when it's two years old, and is milked for about ten months once the calf is born.

Most milk cows are Holsteins—the ones with the black and white spots. They produce the most milk with the lowest proportion of fat. To make milk, cows drink up to fifty gallons of water a day. They eat a mixture of grass, hay, and silage, a feed containing corn cobs and stalks.

Cows are milked twice a day, about twelve hours apart, with a vacuum pump that gently squeezes out the milk—an action similar to that of a sucking calf. Each cow gives about one hundred glasses of milk per day. A small dairy farm has as few as fifty cows; a large one can have up to two thousand.

Milk is warm when it comes out of the cow. Sanitized pipelines carry the milk from the cow to a holding tank, where it is cooled to 45 degrees F. The milk is never touched by hands or exposed to air. Every day or two, a large insulated tank truck stops at the farm to pick up the milk.

The milk is delivered to the dairy, where it's tested in a lab for purity and temperature. The cream (or fat) is then separated from the milk by centrifugal force. The cream is lighter and rises to the top. What is left behind is skimmed milk, or fat-free milk. According to the kind of milk being processed, some of the cream is then added back into the skimmed milk—a small amount for 1% milk, a little more for 2% milk. Whole milk has all the fat added back in; about 3% of whole milk is comprised of fat.

To prevent the cream in the milk from rising to the top, the milk is homogenized. It is pressure-forced through a very small opening that breaks down the fat globules to a uniform (homogenous) size. Once broken down, they are evenly dispersed throughout the milk and can't bond together as cream.

Next, the milk is pasteurized to kill any bacteria that could cause spoilage or disease. It is heated for 15 seconds to 161 degrees F, then rapidly cooled. From there it is routed to a filling machine that pours the milk into containers and delivered by refrigerated trucks to stores, schools, and distributors. The milk travels from the cow to the carton in less than three days.

For more information on the nutrition and processing of milk, visit Whymilk.com or Nationaldairycouncil.org.

The Basics
Temperamental Conditions

In the world of baking, cookies are among the easiest things to make. You don't have to be accomplished in the kitchen to bake a wonderful batch. No special skills are required. All you need are good ingredients, a few basic tools, and a little know-how. It also helps to have the weather on your side.

The Climate

Cookies are little sponges—they absorb moisture from the atmosphere. On a hot, humid day they can turn from crispy-crunchy to soft and limp within hours.

Professional bakers, whether making bread or pastry, change their formulas on a seasonal (and sometimes daily) basis due to fluctuations in heat and humidity, by altering the amount of liquid and/or flour added. Inconsistency is the bane of a baker's reputation.

Grandmothers who bake by "feel" do the same thing. They know their dough. If it needs less liquid on a given day, they hold back. My great-aunts never measured. The recipe was in their heads, and in their hands.

Most cookie recipes will work perfectly when baked in temperate zones from September through mid-June, no matter what the weather. (Meringues are the only exception to this—they don't hold up on rainy days.) Fortunately, the cooler months are when we feel the most compelled to bake.

If you do bake in the sticky heat of summer, and you find your cookies spreading too much or turning soggy the moment they cool, try adding a few extra tablespoons of flour to the recipe. Store the baked cookies in the fridge or freezer rather than at room temperature.

But no matter what the season, be a watchful baker. Baking times can vary, according to the conditions of your oven. Flour, while sitting on your shelf, absorbs moisture from the atmosphere. Some brands of butter contain excess water. Even "large" eggs can vary in size. For the most part, these recipes will work beautifully, exactly as they are. But don't be afraid to make small adjustments now and then.

The Tools

Baking Sheets

Besides the oven, these are probably the single most important tools for successful cookie making. Baking sheets should be large, flat, and made of heavy-gauge aluminum. A good baking sheet will not warp at high temperatures and will distribute the heat evenly. It should measure at least 14 by 17 inches.

Low rims, such as those found on jelly-roll pans, prevent the cookies from baking evenly and make it difficult to remove them. They are useful, however, for toasting nuts; the rim keeps them from rolling off.

Cookies baked on cushioned or Teflon-coated baking sheets generally don't color as well on the bottom or spread as nicely as those baked on heavy aluminum sheets. My favorite baking sheets are made by Vollrath in Sheboygan, Wisconsin.

Cookie Cutters

It's fun to collect them. To have custom cutters made, see Sources, page 25 .

A handy tool for cookie baking is a set of graduated, fluted, round cutters. About nine cutters, ranging in size, come nested in a tin.

Double Boiler

Use a double boiler to cook or melt mixtures that can't tolerate direct heat. That includes chocolate and anything made with eggs, such as custards and meringues.

Most double boilers are made to cook at least a quart of liquid. When cooking small amounts, it is best to rig up your own double boiler. Set a small stainless steel or Pyrex bowl over a small saucepan of **barely simmering** water. Be sure the bottom of the bowl is larger than the opening of the pot. The bottom of the bowl should not touch the water. You need only a half-inch of water to create steam for melting. Once the water boils, turn the heat to low.

If using the double boiler to melt chocolate, be sure the bowl and utensils that touch the chocolate are completely dry (see Melting Chocolate, pages 75–76).

Dough Cutter or Bench Scraper

Professional bakers have little use for sharp knives; the dough cutter is the bakers' tool of choice. It is a dull rectangular metal blade, about 6 inches long, capped with a wooden or plastic handle. Use it to cut the dough into smaller pieces. Also referred to as a bench scraper, this indispensable tool is perfect for scraping the table clean of mess.

| Flexible Metal Palate Knives (or Spatulas) | Sometimes called icing knives, the tip of the blade is rounded and the length of the blade bends for easy maneuvering. An assortment of sizes are used for all sorts of tasks in cookie making. |

Small palate knife   The best way to measure dry ingredients (next to weighing them) is to **scoop and level.** Scoop the measuring cup through the flour (or sugar, or baking powder), then level if off with a small blunt knife. A butter knife works just fine, but a small metal palate knife with a 4-inch blade is a handy tool.

Medium palate knife   Palate knives with blades measuring 8 to 10 inches are used to transfer dough that has been cut with cookie cutters onto the baking sheet. They're also used to transfer warm cookies from the baking sheet to the cooling rack.

Large palate knife   This is an indispensable tool when rolling out cookie dough. It is used to release the dough from the table so that it doesn't stick and cause uneven rolling. The longer the knife, the better. I use a palate knife with a 14-inch blade that I bought in a restaurant/bakery supply store.

| Food Processor | Some cookie doughs are actually better mixed in the food processor. Almond macaroons are a good example, as are biscotti and sandy shortbread. The food processor is especially handy for quickly chopping nuts, dried fruit, and chocolate. Pulse the machine, rather than running it continuously, so that the nuts don't become oily. |

| Ice-Cream Scoops | These are very handy for forming dough into perfectly even balls. The procedure is quick and results are consistent. The spring-release type of scoop enables you to drop the cookies easily onto the baking sheet. The most frequently used sizes are 1 1/8 inches, 1 1/2 inches, and 2 1/2 inches in diameter. |

| Measuring Cups & Spoons | It's convenient to have two sets of each: one set for measuring wet ingredients, the other for dry.
Liquid measuring cups are simply pitchers with a little extra room at the top to prevent the liquid from spilling—the measure is no different. Don't use them to measure dry ingredients; it's difficult to be accurate if you can't scoop and level off the cup. |

Microwave Oven

I love to melt butter and chocolate in the microwave. There's no need to fine-chop the chocolate as in a double boiler; even large chunks melt rather evenly. Also, there's no danger of water getting into the bowl and ruining the whole batch of chocolate, as there is with a double boiler. Whether melting chocolate in the microwave or double boiler, check and stir frequently: high heat burns chocolate. (See Melting Chocolate, pages 75–76.) Keep a variety of Pyrex or microwave-safe containers and bowls on hand to melt large and small quantities of chocolate and butter.

The microwave is also wonderful for softening cold butter and hard dough. Heat for 10 to 15 seconds on medium power. Check in 10-second increments so that they don't oversoften.

Mixer

Until this century, perfectly wonderful cookies were made without the aid of electric mixers. A strong arm, a wooden spoon, and time were all that were required. Unequipped individuals and backwoods bakers can still make dough in this fashion. Have all ingredients at room temperature; it makes for quicker and easier mixing.

A handheld mixer is the next step up. The newer models are powerful. They move through the dough quickly and are easy to clean. Handheld mixers are relatively inexpensive. It may be worth investing in a new one if yours is the old style.

The stand (or tabletop) mixer is a luxurious tool; your hands are free while the mixer does the work. The flat beater, or paddle attachment, is used to cream the butter and sugar. The wire whip attachment aerates light mixes such as meringue. Egg whites whipped in a stand mixer will attain more volume than those made with a handheld mixer. Stand mixers are expensive, but well worth the investment if you love to bake.

Mixing Bowls

Keep a variety of stainless steel or Pyrex bowls on hand. The larger ones are used as mixing bowls for a handheld electric mixer. The smaller ones hold nuts, chocolate chips, and other ingredients. Purchase sets of nesting bowls—they look good and save space in the cupboard.

Oven Thermometer

The oven temperature must be accurate, or the cookies will not bake properly. A hot oven will crisp the exterior of a cookie too quickly, preventing it from spreading and leaving the inside underdone. A slow oven will dry out the cookie. To make sure the oven setting agrees with the temperature inside, calibrate your oven. Rather than spending money on an expensive service call, telephone the manufacturer. In most cases they can talk you through the calibrating process. It's very simple to do.

Even so, I leave a thermometer in the oven at all times. In fact, I use two. They don't always agree, but I get a consensus. Hang the thermometer from the middle rack in the oven—don't place it on the oven floor. Be sure the oven is fully preheated before baking the first tray of cookies.

Parchment Paper

This silicon-treated paper is a baker's best friend. It saves time and mess. You don't have to worry about greasing the baking sheet, and clean-up is a snap. Purchase it on a roll in the supermarket or a housewares store.

Parchment paper will slow down the baking process a little. It also reduces the spreading of cookies. If a recipe calls for a buttered baking sheet and you use parchment, be aware that your results may vary.

Pastry and Bench Brushes

The occasional cookie recipe requires a pastry brush. It's used for painting water, egg wash, or melted butter on dough, and for washing down the sides of a pot when cooking sugar syrup on the stove. A 1-inch-wide, flat brush works fine for most tasks.

A bench brush is used to sweep excess flour off rolled dough. It is usually about 8 inches wide with long, soft bristles. If you're making a lot of rolled cookies at holiday time, it's a terrific tool to have.

Pastry Bags and Tips

Perfectly round cookies can be piped out of pastry bags fitted with round or decorative star-shaped tips. Cut the end off the bag so that it fits the tip you are inserting, then drop the tip down through the bag. An 18-inch bag is a good size for piping cookie batter.

Clear plastic disposable pastry bags are handy—they can be washed and reused a number of times, and then disposed of before they get stinky. Use a new bag when piping out meringues to assure there is no residual butter inside.

Rolling Pin

The type of rolling pin you use is a personal choice. Some people prefer the solid dowel type of pin; others find it easier to use a rolling pin with handles on each end. For cookie baking, I find a 12-inch ball-bearing wooden rolling pin works just fine. If a film of dough collects on the pin as you roll, stand it on end and wipe it down with your hand or a paper towel.

Rubber Spatula and Rubber Scraper	Scrape the sides and bottom of the mixing bowl frequently—that's the only way to get an evenly mixed dough. Use a **sturdy** rubber spatula. Professionals use white rubber spatulas with strong white plastic handles. They come in three sizes. The large spatula, about 14 inches long, is handy for scraping down the sides of a stand mixing bowl. The medium one works well for almost everything else. Little spatulas are handy for scraping chocolate and melted butter out of small bowls.
	If the dough is heavy and stiff, you can get better leverage with a flexible plastic hand scraper. It's either kidney-shaped or rectangular with a curved edge. There is no handle—it fits right in your palm. The flat side is used to scrape the mess off the table; the rounded edge is used to scrape down the bowl.
Ruler	I always keep a ruler in the kitchen—it's useful for measuring dough. If a piece of dough is rolled larger than the recipe specifies, the yield will be higher but the cookies will be smaller. They'll dry out as they bake in the oven. A metal ruler is better than wood in the kitchen, because it's easier to wash and dry.
Scale	Americans bake by measure; Europeans (and professionals both here and abroad) bake by weight. Weighing is more accurate. A cup of flour can contain anywhere from 3 to 5 ounces, depending on how settled and compressed it is.
	I use a scale for weighing chocolate, or for dividing a dough or batter in half. Digital scales are easy to use, because they usually have a feature that returns the scale to zero whenever you choose, so you can negate the weight of the container. Choose a scale that weighs in increments of one-quarter ounce. A scale that can weigh 5 pounds is sufficient; 10 pounds is even better.
Sifter/Strainer	I find most flour sifters small, cumbersome, and hard to clean. I prefer to use a medium-fine mesh strainer with a handle. Rest the strainer over a bowl and dump in the dry ingredients. Shake them out over the bowl or onto a piece of waxed paper.
Timer	There's nothing more frustrating than burning a tray of cookies; it's such a waste. An hour timer is a handy reminder—the louder and more relentless the better.
Wire Cooling Racks	Cookies can get soggy if they aren't properly cooled. Large cooling racks, the same size as the baking sheets, are mandatory for cookie baking. It's convenient to have two racks so that there is room to cool a large batch of cookies.

The Main Ingredients

Using Ingredients

Measuring   Short of weighing them on a scale, the most accurate way to measure dry ingredients is to **scoop and level.** Dip the measuring cup or spoon into the flour, sugar, baking powder, or whatever. Scoop it up, then level it off with the blunt edge of a knife.

When a recipe calls for an amount for which there is no exact measuring tool, combine smaller measures. For example, to measure 3/4 cup, combine 1/2 cup of the ingredient with another 1/4 cup. To measure 6 tablespoons, use 1/4 cup with two additional tablespoons. Two-thirds cup is most easily measured by using a 1/3 cup measure twice.

To avoid making a mess, I like to transfer dry ingredients to wide-mouth containers with lids. Tupperware-type plastic containers are good for ingredients that come in 1-pound boxes such as brown or powdered sugar. For larger canisters to hold flour and white sugar, I use clear plastic boxes with tight-fitting lids found in restaurant/bakery supply stores. They look nice lined up on the shelf.

Room Temperature   Unless the recipe specifies otherwise, have all ingredients at room temperature (65 to 75 degrees) before you begin. Butter should be malleable and soft enough to yield to gentle pressure. Softened butter is easily beaten into a light and airy mass that can absorb the sugar. Cold butter is dense and non-absorbent. A quick way to soften butter is to slice it into tablespoon pieces, and warm it in the microwave for a few seconds (see Microwave Oven, page 15). Cold eggs will curdle the butter and sugar. Let them sit outside the refrigerator for a few hours before you bake. If you forget, take the chill off the eggs by placing them in a bowl of warm water for a few minutes.

Butter and Eggs   Use unsalted butter. It allows you to control the amount of salt you add to the recipe. Large eggs are always called for, because they are a standard size. The wrong size egg makes the dough wet or too dry.

Flour   Flour contains protein and starch. Depending on the breed of wheat, and the soil and climate in which it is grown, certain flours contain more or less protein or starch. Hard wheat flour, or bread flour, contains more protein. It has the ability to form gluten—a strong elastic web of protein strands that allows the bread to rise and hold gas like a balloon. Soft wheat flour, or pastry flour, contains more starch. It doesn't have the "strength" of bread flour, so it's better for tender pastries such as cake and biscuits. All-purpose flour falls between the two. It can be used to make either bread or pastry, hence its name. It's the best flour for making most cookies. I get the best results with white, bleached all-purpose flour (unless the recipe specifies otherwise). If you use a different kind of flour, you may have to adjust slightly the liquid in the recipe.

Baking Powder and Soda   These chemical leaveners are responsible for lifting and spreading the cookie dough in the oven. They must be fresh and active to do their job. To test baking powder, drop half a teaspoon into a cup of warm water. It should fizz vigorously. To test baking soda, add a few drops of lemon juice or vinegar to a small amount. If active, it will bubble and fizz.

Nuts and Dried Fruit   Only fresh and tasty will do. No one will want a second cookie made with tasteless nuts or dried fruit that is as hard as pellets. Purchase these ingredients in a store where they sell a large quantity—a health food store or busy gourmet supermarket.

To keep nuts fresh, refrigerate them in an airtight container. Crisp them up in a 350-degree oven, for about 10 minutes. Let them cool to room temperature before adding them to the dough. **Unblanched** means that the paper-thin, brown outer husks are left on the nuts; **blanched** means the skins are removed.

Vanilla Extract   Use the pure stuff; there is no substitute. Vanilla extract is made from the pods of an orchid plant. It is highly aromatic, and has a way of rounding out the taste of almost any cookie. Imitation vanilla is extracted from wood-pulp by-products. It doesn't approach the aroma and flavor of the real thing.

The Techniques

Mixing the Dough

Creaming Butter and Sugar   Most cookie recipes begin by combining soft-ened butter and sugar into a creamy mass. This can be done with a wooden spoon, a handheld mixer, or the paddle attachment of a stand mixer. The more you mix them together, the lighter and fluffier they become. Some recipes call for creaming the butter and sugar just until they are well combined. Follow the recipe. Over-aerating the mix can cause certain doughs to spread too much in the oven.

Adding the Eggs   If the recipe calls for more than one egg, add the eggs one at a time, allowing each to be absorbed before adding the next. Use a rubber spat-ula to scrape the bottom of the bowl between additions.

Whipping   To incorporate air into light ingredients such as egg whites with sugar, mix them using a whisk, a handheld mixer, or the whip attachment of a stand mixer. Meringues are one of the few cookies that are whipped. For more detailed instructions on making them, see Mastering Meringue: The Rules, page 102.

Combining Dry Ingredients   Once the flour, leavener, salt, and spices have been sifted or whisked in a bowl, the dry ingredients need to be added to the mix. To prevent making a big mess, and to assure that all the dry ingredients make it into the mixing bowl, dump them onto a piece of waxed paper, lift it up by the ends, and shake them into the mix.

Adding the Flour   Flour contains protein; when that protein comes in contact with moisture, strands of gluten are formed. As these strands are agitated—by stir-ring or kneading—they form a strong, elastic web. This web is good for bread, as it allows the dough to rise and expand. It's not good for cookies, however—it makes them tough. When adding flour to the mix, agitate it as little as possible so as not to activate the gluten. Do this by stirring in the flour by hand, or on low speed using an electric mixer. Mix just until the flour is absorbed into the dough.

Scraping the Bowl   Don't let lumps of butter or clumps of flour lurk on the bottom of the mixing bowl; they belong in the batter. Scrape around the sides and along the bottom of the bowl frequently with a rubber spatula to thoroughly incorporate the ingredients. Scrape down the bowl when creaming the butter and sugar, once again after adding the eggs, and a final time after adding the dry ingredients. When you bring up the unmixed stuff, beat for a few seconds to combine it into the mix before adding the next ingredient.

Forming the Cookies

Scooped   For speed and consistency, professional bakers use an ice-cream scoop to dish out firm cookie dough. I keep a variety of spring-release scoops on hand for both large and small cookies. A rounded scoop gives a different-size cookie than a level scoop. Follow the recipe. If you make the balls of dough too large, you'll get fewer cookies from the batch and they'll take longer to bake.

Dropped   This is the way in which most people form chocolate chip cookies. Medium-firm dough is dropped off a spoon onto the baking sheet. Another spoon is used to nudge the batter off the first spoon. This technique is slow and cumbersome, and usually yields cookies of varying sizes. Try using an ice-cream scoop for doughs that you normally drop from a spoon.

Piped   Loose doughs or stiff batters can be piped onto the baking sheet from a piping bag. The technique is quick and fun, and each dollop looks exactly like the last (after a little practice). To fill the bag, drop the tip down into the bag, turn back a cuff, then fill the bag using a rubber spatula. For easy maneuvering, support the bag inside an empty water glass while you fill it. Once the bag is two-thirds full, twist the top to close it. Grasp the bag with one hand over the twist; use your other hand to support the tip of the bag. Hold the pastry bag upright at least 1/2 inch above the baking sheet, depending on the size of the cookie. Squeeze and release. With a little practice, you'll have perfect little piped-out cookies.

Hand-Formed   Cookies that are individually shaped by hand, such as balls, crescents, or logs, should all be the same size. Professional bakers have a trick to accomplish this. Roll the dough into an even log, then slice the log into small even pieces. Each of these pieces can then be formed into the shape you want.

Rolled   See Rolling the Dough, page 126.

Preparing the Baking Sheets

An easy way to lightly grease the baking sheets is to smear them with the wrapper from the stick of butter, or smear the stick of butter itself across the sheets.

Don't place cookie dough on a warm baking sheet—the butter in the mix will melt, affecting the texture of the cookie. To cool a baking sheet quickly, run it under cold water and dry it thoroughly. Or better yet, have at least three baking sheets on hand so you can prepare one while another is in the oven and the third is cooling.

Unless a baking sheet is particularly burned or crusty, simply wipe it clean with a paper towel between bakings.

Baking

The first instruction in a recipe is one of the most important: **Preheat the oven.** This takes at least 15 minutes. Don't be impatient. A too-low oven temperature can result in dried-out cookies (they take too long to bake) or cookies that don't rise or spread properly.

Except when making meringues (which are essentially dried in the oven), I bake one tray of cookies at a time. I find they bake evenly and quickly. If you want to bake two trays at once, switch and rotate them halfway through. Keep in mind they'll take a little longer to bake.

Place the baking sheet on a rack in the middle of the oven. If you're baking two trays of cookies, arrange the racks as close to the center as possible without crowding them too much.

Storing

Cookies are generally quick and easy to make. In most cases, you can whip up a batch on the spot—or just hours ahead of serving them. With the exception of twice-baked cookies such as biscotti and mandelbrot, or very crisp ones such as sugar cookies or gingerbread (which all stay crisp and tasty for days), cookies are almost always best eaten on the day they're made.

To store baked cookies, be sure they are completely cool first. Don't mix different flavors and textures in one container. Crisp cookies will become soggy; the flavors will mix and mingle and nothing will taste as it should.

Wrapping Cookies   Plastic containers with tight-fitting lids can be used to store most cookies, but occasionally they make cookies limp. Some cookies, such as chocolate chip, may fare better in cookie jars, or left out on cooling racks overnight. Cookies can also be packaged in waxed paper that's covered tightly with foil.

Freezing Cookies   If you live in the humid Northeast (or the rainy Northwest, or the muggy South, or even the stormy Midwest), cookies can turn soft quickly. Freezing cookies keeps them fresher. Wrap them tightly in aluminum foil, then seal them in zip-lock bags, pressing all the air out. Theoretically you can freeze them for up to three months, but I think they're best eaten within two weeks.

Let the cookies thaw, partially unwrapped, at room temperature, or thaw and warm them in the oven at 350 degrees F for a few minutes. Place them on wire racks to cool as if they're fresh baked. They may not be quite as good as just-made, but they'll be mighty good.

Refrigerating and Freezing Dough   To save time, and still have fresh-baked cookies on hand, refrigerate the dough for a few days, or freeze it for up to two weeks. Wrap it well in plastic wrap.

Dough that contains no leavening, such as shortbread and butter cookie dough, can be refrigerated quite successfully for up to three days. Dough that contains baking powder or soda will lose its lift within two days.

Let frozen dough thaw overnight in the refrigerator, unless the recipe specifies otherwise. If the dough cracks when you roll it, it's too cold. Divide it in sections and let it sit at room temperature, covered, until malleable but not too soft—15 to 20 minutes.

When making scooped or dropped cookies with dough that has been refrigerated, let it come to room temperature until it has the consistency of fresh-made dough. The microwave can be used judiciously to speed up the softening. Use low power and check the dough every few seconds so that it doesn't get too soft.

Sources

To order ingredients and equipment by mail, phone, or E-mail, contact:

The Baker's Catalog
King Arthur Flour
P. O. Box 876
Norwich, Vermont 05055
www.kingarthurflour.com
(800) 827-6836
Baking tools and ingredients; emphasis on bread-baking, no cookie sheets

The Broadway Panhandler
477 Broome Street
New York, New York 10013
(212) 966-3434
Baking equipment including Vollrath cookie sheets, food colors, and decorating tools

HammerSong
221 S. Potomac Street
Boonsboro, Maryland 21713
(301) 432-4320
Custom-made solid-backed cutters with intricate inside detail, plus a catalog of 80 stock designs

**The New York Cake &
Baking Distributor**
56 West 22nd Street
New York, New York 10010
www.nycakesupplies.com
(800) 942-2539
Decorating sugars, food colors, Royal Icing mix, cookie stamps and cutters, baking and decorating tools

Parrish's
225 West 146th Street
Gardena, California 90248
(800) 736-8443
Custom-made stainless steel cookie cutters in simple shapes

Williams-Sonoma
100 Northpoint
San Francisco, California 94133
(800) 541-2233
www.williams-sonoma.com
Baking tools and some ingredients

www.CookieRecipe.com
Extensive listing of recipes and equipment

Chocolate Chip Cookies

About Chocolate Chip Cookies

Chocolate chip cookies are best eaten warm from the oven, while you're standing in front of an open refrigerator—guzzling milk straight from the carton.

They are the most American of cookies, created in the 1930s (so the story goes) when Ruth Wakefield, owner of the Toll House Inn in Whitman, Massachusetts, ran out of nuts to put in her butter cookies. She resourcefully chopped up a bar of semisweet chocolate and added it to the dough. The morsels didn't melt and swirl in the dough as she had hoped, but her customers loved them nonetheless and the concept caught on quickly. Nestle's began scoring chocolate bars for easy breaking, and printing her recipe on the package. By 1939, the company was manufacturing semisweet bits sold by the bagful. A few years later they bought the Toll House name.

Nestle's Toll House Morsels are no longer the only chip on the block. Buy a few brands and taste them side by side; you will be able to detect a clear difference between them. Some are unpleasantly waxy, grainy, or just plain bland. While Toll House still stands up quite well in comparison, Guittard makes a lovely chip, as does Tropical Source, which can be found in health food stores.

With the current craze for chocolate chunks rather than chips in the cookie, we've come full circle to Mrs. Wakefield's original version. Semisweet chocolate has a pleasing bitter undertone that is the perfect foil for this buttery sweet cookie. High-quality chocolate bars made by Lindt, Valrhona, and Ghirardelli, to name a few, are available in specialty gourmet food stores and some supermarkets. The 3- or 4-ounce bars are scored for easy breaking.

It is the opinion of most (myself included) that chocolate chip cookies call for nuts. Without them, the cookies are flat. You can't go wrong with pecans—the all-American nut (indigenous to our land) and one of the sweetest. But there is ample opportunity for divergence. Hazelnuts, macadamias, peanuts, and walnuts are terrific in combination with semisweet, milk, or white chocolate.

Ever wonder why your chocolate chip cookies don't look quite like those in the magazines, with gleaming melty chips and chunks peeking through the golden crust? Take a tip from the pros: those chunks are carefully placed. To make your cookies picture perfect, mix the chips or chunks and nuts into the dough, holding back a scant fourth the amount. Once the cookies are dropped onto the baking sheet, stick a few pieces from the reserve on the tops and sides of each ball of dough. It takes a little more time (kids can get involved in this project), but the visuals are worth it. It's also a way for the outside of the cookie to tell the story of what's inside.

There's nothing like biting into a crunchy cookie with warm, oozy chunks of chocolate inside. Chocolate chip cookies are so easy to make, there is really no reason to bake them ahead. They are never as good stored or frozen as they are the day they come out of the oven. Chocolate chips and chunks will remain soft and runny for hours, even when the cookies are completely cool.

There are no special skills or fancy equipment required to make chocolate chip cookies. It's a terrific way to introduce small children to baking—you don't even need an electric mixer. A sturdy rubber spatula, a mixing bowl, and a few bars of excellent chocolate will make you a hero or heroine in your kid's classroom or a cherished houseguest on your next weekend visit.

Quick Tips on Chocolate Chips

◎ Soften the butter at room temperature, or briefly in the microwave, just until it yields to light pressure. Overly softened butter will cause the cookies to spread too much in the oven.

◎ Don't overbeat the butter and sugar. Mix them until well combined, but not light and fluffy. Overmixing will cause the cookies to spread too much.

◎ Don't sift the flour. On hot, humid days, add an extra tablespoon or two of flour to the mix to prevent the cookies from going flat.

◎ Break, rather than cut, 3- or 4-ounce chocolate bars into 1/2-inch chunks. A knife creates too many small shards and crumbles.

◎ Milk and white chocolate **chips** tend to be cloyingly sweet. It is better to use high-quality white or milk chocolate **bars** broken into chunks, rather than chips.

◎ Six ounces of chips measure 1 **level** cup; 6 ounces of chunks measure 1 **rounded** cup. When using chunks, go by the weight called for in a recipe rather than the measure. You don't need a scale. Chocolate bars are scored into small squares. Just read the weight on the wrapper and figure out how many squares there are per ounce.

© For a cookie more densely populated with chocolate, feel free to increase the amount of chips in the following recipes from 1 cup to 1 1/3 cup, or the amount of chocolate chunks from 6 to 8 ounces.

© Toasted nuts are tastier than raw. Even pecans and walnuts will benefit from 10 minutes in the oven at 350 degrees F. Make sure they're completely cool before adding them to the dough.

© Most chocolate chip dough is just dry enough to allow you to roll walnut-size balls gently and gingerly between your palms. If the dough sticks, wet the palms of your hands.

© A quick way to form perfectly round mounds of dough is to use an ice-cream scoop measuring 1 to 1 1/2 inches in diameter. Level the dough off across the top before dropping it onto the baking sheet. You can also shape and drop the dough using two spoons.

© To make large cookies, use an ice-cream scoop measuring about 2 inches in diameter, leveling the dough off across the top before dropping it onto the baking sheet. Using the palm of your hand, press each mound down to a thickness of about 1/2 inch. (Wet your hand if the dough sticks.) Bake the cookies for 12 to 14 minutes. You'll get about half the amount of large cookies from a batch of dough.

© Use ungreased baking sheets. You can fit fourteen cookies on a 14-by-17-inch baking sheet by arranging them in alternating rows of three and four across.

© Cookies bake best one tray at a time in the oven. If you need to reuse a baking sheet, allow it to cool and wipe it clean between batches.

© Bake the cookies until the edges are golden brown and appear done; the centers may look slightly underbaked. This could take anywhere from 9 to 14 minutes, depending on your oven. The cookies will continue to darken on the baking sheet once they are removed from the oven. Let them remain on the hot tray until sturdy enough to transfer to a cooling rack—4 to 5 minutes. The cookies will deflate as they cool.

◎ To make a larger batch of cookies, any of the recipes in this chapter may be doubled.

◎ To save time, make the dough ahead and chill it for up to two days in the refrigerator, or freeze it for up to a week. When ready to bake, let the dough come to room temperature, then scoop and bake.

◎ In cool, dry weather, chocolate chip cookies fare quite well overnight when left out in the open on a plate or wire rack, or they can be stored for up to three days in a tin or cookie jar. Airtight plastic containers tend to make chocolate chip cookies limp; hot or muggy weather will make them soggy. To crisp and freshen baked cookies, arrange them on baking sheets and heat in a 350-degree F oven for about 5 minutes, then cool on wire racks.

◎ If you **must** bake ahead, freeze the cookies for up to two weeks wrapped in foil and sealed in plastic bags (see Freezing Cookies, page 24). Chocolate chip cookies are even quite tasty eaten frozen, if you're too impatient to defrost. To simulate just-baked cookies, thaw them at room temperature, warm them in a 350-degree F oven, and cool the cookies on wire racks.

The Classic Chocolate Chip

4 ounces (1 stick) unsalted
  butter, softened

6 tablespoons granulated
  sugar

6 tablespoons packed light
  brown sugar

1/4 teaspoon salt

1 1/2 teaspoons vanilla
  extract

1 large egg

1 cup plus 2 tablespoons
  all-purpose flour

1/2 teaspoon baking soda

1 cup (6 ounces) chocolate
  chunks or chips

1 cup (about 3 1/2 ounces)
  large pecan or walnut
  pieces, or any nut you
  prefer

About 2 1/2 dozen cookies

This is adapted from Mrs. Wakefield's original recipe. It's pretty much the perfect chocolate chip cookie: soft, chewy, crisp, and crunchy all at once. She dissolved the baking soda first in a 1/4 teaspoon of warm water. You get equally good results by whisking the dry baking soda into the flour.

1 Preheat oven to 375 degrees F.

2 In a medium bowl, using an electric mixer, beat the butter, sugars, salt, and vanilla until well combined. Beat in the egg. Scrape down the bowl using a rubber spatula, and beat for a few more seconds.

3 In a small bowl, whisk together the flour and baking soda. Add the dry ingredients to the wet mixture and mix on low speed just until absorbed. Combine the chocolate chunks and nuts in a small bowl and stir into the dough.

4 Shape the dough into 1 1/2-inch balls and drop them about 3 inches apart onto ungreased baking sheets. For perfectly uniform cookies, scoop the dough using a 1 1/2-inch-diameter ice-cream scoop, leveling the dough off across the top before dropping onto the baking sheets. Bake for 9 to 12 minutes, or until the edges are golden. Let sit for 5 minutes, then transfer to wire racks to cool completely.

Cookie

Thin and Chewy CCCs

5 ounces (1 1/4 sticks) unsalted
    butter, softened
1/4 cup granulated sugar
1/2 cup packed light brown
    sugar
1/4 teaspoon salt
1 1/2 teaspoons vanilla
    extract
1 large egg
1 cup plus 2 tablespoons
    all-purpose flour
1/2 teaspoon baking soda
1 cup (6 ounces) chocolate
    chunks or chips
1 cup nuts

About 2 1/2 dozen cookies

NOTE: In hot, humid weather, reduce the amount of butter to 1 stick (4 ounces) to prevent these cookies from spreading too much.

If you crave the buttery, soft, chewy cookies sold in franchise chocolate chip boutiques, here you have them. They puff up in the oven, then collapse as they cool, forming an unevenly wrinkled surface. The dough contains a little extra butter and twice as much brown sugar as white, so they stay soft and chewy.

1 Preheat oven to 375 degrees F.

2 In a medium bowl, using an electric mixer, beat the butter, sugars, salt, and vanilla until well combined. Beat in the egg. Scrape down the bowl using a rubber spatula and beat for a few more seconds.

3 In a small bowl, whisk together the flour and baking soda. Add the dry ingredients to the wet mixture on low speed and mix just until absorbed. Combine the chocolate chunks and nuts in a small bowl and stir into the dough.

4 Shape the dough into 1 1/2-inch balls and drop them about 3 inches apart onto ungreased baking sheets. For perfectly uniform cookies, scoop the dough using a 1 1/2-inch-diameter ice-cream scoop, leveling the dough off across the top before dropping onto the baking sheets. Bake for about 10 to 12 minutes, or until the edges are golden. Let sit for 5 minutes, then transfer to wire racks to cool completely.

Thick and Chewy CCCs

2 ounces (1/2 stick) unsalted
    butter, softened

6 tablespoons granulated
    sugar

6 tablespoons packed light
    brown sugar

1/4 teaspoon salt

1 1/2 teaspoons vanilla
    extract

1 large egg

1 cup plus 2 tablespoons
    all-purpose flour

1/2 teaspoon baking soda

1 cup (6 ounces) chocolate
    chunks or chips

1 cup nuts

About 2 dozen cookies

NOTE: For a thinner cookie,
use the palm of your hand
to flatten each ball, wetting
your hand if the dough sticks.
Be careful not to overbake
or they will lose their chewy
texture.

These have a little something to please everyone: soft and chewy centers, crisp edges, cracked tops, and the substantial biteful of a thick cookie. The dough contains less butter than the standard recipe, which prevents the cookies from spreading too much in the oven.

1 Preheat oven to 375 degrees F.

2 In a medium bowl, using an electric mixer, beat the butter, sugars, salt, and vanilla until well combined. Beat in the egg. Scrape down the bowl using a rubber spatula and beat for a few more seconds.

3 In a small bowl, whisk together the flour and baking soda. Add the dry ingredients to the wet mixture and mix on low speed just until absorbed. Combine the chocolate chunks and nuts in a small bowl and stir into the dough.

4 Shape the dough into 1 1/2-inch balls and drop them about 3 inches apart onto ungreased baking sheets. For perfectly uniform cookies, scoop the dough using a 1 1/2-inch-diameter ice-cream scoop, leveling the dough off across the top before dropping onto the baking sheets. Bake for 10 to 12 minutes, or until the edges are golden. Let sit for 5 minutes, then transfer to wire racks to cool completely.

Crisp and Crunchy CCCs

8 ounces (2 sticks) unsalted
 butter, softened

1 1/4 cups granulated sugar

1/4 cup packed light brown
 sugar

1/2 teaspoon salt

1 tablepoon vanilla extract

1 large egg

2 1/2 cups all-purpose flour

1 teaspoon baking soda

2 cups (12 ounces) chocolate
 chunks or chips

2 cups nuts

About 4 1/2 dozen cookies

NOTE: This recipe makes a
larger quantity of cookies
because it's inconvenient to
follow a recipe calling for 1/2
egg. If you do want to halve
the recipe, the easiest way to
divide an egg is to crack it in
a small cup, beat it lightly
with a fork, then divide it

Eat these cookies in bed and you'll end up with crumbs in the sheets. They're more like the packaged cookies sold commercially—fairly thick, crisp, and crunchy, with small cracks across the top. Less egg, extra flour, and more white sugar than brown makes them that way.

If you want a thinner cookie, flatten the balls of dough with the palm of your hand. The cookies take less time to bake and are larger that way, but they lose that nice cracked professional-looking surface.

1 Preheat oven to 375 degrees F.

2 In a medium bowl, using an electric mixer, beat the butter, sugars, salt, and vanilla until well combined. Beat in the egg. Scrape down the bowl using a rubber spatula and beat for a few more seconds.

3 In a small bowl, whisk together the flour and baking soda. Add the dry ingredients to the wet mixture and mix on low speed just until absorbed. Combine the chocolate chunks and nuts in a small bowl and stir into the dough.

4 Shape the dough into 1 1/2-inch balls and drop them about 3 inches apart onto ungreased baking sheets. For perfectly uniform cookies, scoop the dough using a 1 1/2-inch-diameter ice-cream scoop, leveling the dough off across the top before dropping onto the baking sheets. For thinner cookies, use the upper palm of your hand to flatten each ball into a 1/2-inch thick disk. (If the dough sticks, wet your hand.) Bake for 10 to 13 minutes, or until golden. Let sit for 5 minutes, then transfer to wire racks to cool completely.

evenly into two cups by sight
or tablespoon by tablespoon.
If you own a kitchen scale,
simply divide into two cups
and weigh.

Variation:
Anyway You Like Them

For a flavor twist, add one of the following to the CCC recipe of your choice.

1 tablespoon finely grated orange zest (especially good with milk chocolate chunks)

1 cup coarsely chopped dates

1 cup dark or golden raisins

Variation:
Blonde on Blonde CCCs

White chocolate chunks and macadamia nuts are the platinum version of chocolate chip cookies. White chocolate chips tend to be cloyingly sweet; instead, use high-quality white chocolate bars broken into half-inch pieces. Follow the instructions for making, forming, and baking the CCC recipe of your choice, but substitute white chocolate for dark chocolate, and add macadamia nuts according to amounts called for in the recipe.

white chocolate chunks

macadamia nuts, coarsely chopped

Double Trouble

Chocolate Chip Cookies

4 ounces (1 stick) unsalted
   butter, softened

3/4 cup granulated sugar

1/4 teaspoon salt

1 teaspoon vanilla extract

1/3 cup unsweetened cocoa
   (preferably Dutch-
   process)

1 large egg

1 cup all-purpose flour

1/2 teaspoon baking soda

1 cup (6 ounces) bittersweet
   chocolate chunks or chips

1 cup (3 1/2 ounces) large
   pecan pieces

About 28 cookies

Dark and chewy with a deep chocolate flavor, these lumpy, bumpy cookies are filled with large pecan pieces and spotted with a mosaic of dark chocolate chunks. Use high-quality chocolate bars broken into half-inch irregular pieces.

Make your own Double Trouble. Use this recipe as a jumping-off place to customize your chocolatey chocolate chip cookie. Substitute hazelnuts or macadamias for the pecans. Use white chocolate chunks instead of semisweet, or add milk chocolate chips.

1. Preheat oven to 350 degrees F.

2. In a medium bowl, using an electric mixer, beat the butter, sugar, salt, and vanilla until well combined. Beat in the cocoa, then the egg. Scrape down the bowl using a rubber spatula and beat for a few more seconds.

3. In a small bowl, whisk together the flour and baking soda. Add the dry ingredients to the wet mixture, and mix on low speed just until absorbed. Combine the chocolate chunks and nuts in a small bowl and stir into the dough.

4. Shape the dough into 1 1/2-inch balls and drop them about 3 inches apart onto ungreased baking sheets. For perfectly uniform cookies, scoop the dough using a 1 1/2-inch-diameter ice-cream scoop, leveling the dough off across the top before dropping onto the baking sheets. Bake for 10 minutes. Let sit for 5 minutes, then transfer to wire racks to cool completely.

Variation: More Double Trouble

Let the following combinations inspire you to create your own Double Trouble, using the proportions given above (1 cup of chunks or chips with 1 cup of nuts per one full recipe).

White chocolate chunks with pecans and/or dried cranberries

White chocolate chunks with macadamia nuts, toasted and coarsely chopped

Milk chocolate chunks with dry roasted peanuts

Dark chocolate chunks with walnuts

Half white and half dark chocolate chunks with walnuts or pecans

Mocha Marble CCCs

1 tablespoon instant coffee

1/2 teaspoon hot water

4 ounces (1 stick) unsalted

butter, softened

1/2 cup packed light brown

sugar

1/4 cup granulated sugar

1/4 teaspoon salt

1 teaspoon vanilla extract

1 egg

1 cup plus 2 tablespoons

all-purpose flour

1/2 teaspoon baking soda

2 1/2 tablespoons unsweet-

ened cocoa (preferably

Dutch-process)

1 1/3 cups (8 ounces)

semisweet chocolate

chunks

1 cup (3 1/2 ounces) large

pecan pieces

About 24 to 28 cookies

Two harmonious flavors—coffee and chocolate—and two contrasting colors—black and tan—are marbled together in one chocolate chip cookie.

The entire dough is flavored with coffee and divided in half. Cocoa is then stirred into half the mix. A pinch of both is used to form each cookie, which is chock-full of dark chocolate chunks and pecans.

1 Preheat oven to 375 degrees F. In a cup, dissolve the instant coffee in the hot water.

2 In a medium bowl, using an electric mixer, beat the butter, sugars, salt, and vanilla until well combined. Beat in the egg and dissolved coffee. Scrape down the bowl using a rubber spatula and beat for a few more seconds.

3 In a small bowl, whisk together the flour and baking soda. Add the dry ingredients to the wet mixture and mix on low speed just until absorbed. Divide the mix in half and sift the cocoa into one part; use a rubber spatula to thoroughly incorporate. Combine the chocolate chunks and nuts in a small bowl and stir half into each of the two doughs.

4 Using about 1/2 tablespoon of each dough, combine them into balls and drop them onto baking sheets. For perfectly uniform cookies, scoop some of each dough using a 1 1/2-inch-diameter ice-cream scoop, leveling the dough off across the top before dropping onto the baking sheets about 3 inches apart. Bake for about 10 minutes, until the cookies puff and the edges of the lighter-colored dough begin to color. (You'll have to look very closely to see the color change.) Do not overbake. Let sit for 4 minutes, then transfer to wire racks to cool completely.

Peanut Butter CCCs

4 ounces (1 stick) unsalted
butter, softened

2/3 cup creamy peanut butter

3/4 cup packed dark brown
sugar

1/4 cup granulated sugar

1 teaspoon vanilla extract

1 egg

1 cup all-purpose flour

1/2 teaspoon baking soda

1 1/3 cups (8 ounces)
semisweet chocolate
chunks or chips

1/2 cup (2 1/2 ounces) dry-
roasted peanuts, coarsely
chopped

About 32 cookies

In popular American cuisine, the beloved combination of peanut butter and chocolate is right up there with roast turkey and cranberry sauce.

The classic peanut butter cookie is thick, crunchy, and a bit clunky. These cookies pack a powerful peanut punch, but have the texture and appearance of chocolate chip cookies: not terribly thick, with soft centers and crunchy edges. Add either milk chocolate or semisweet chocolate chunks or chips. Peanut Butter CCCs holler for a tall, cold glass of milk.

1 Preheat oven to 375 degrees F.

2 In a medium bowl, using an electric mixer, beat the butter, peanut butter, sugars, and vanilla until well combined. Beat in the egg. Scrape down the bowl using a rubber spatula and beat for a few more seconds.

3 In a small bowl, whisk together the flour and baking soda. Add the dry ingredients to the wet mixture and mix on low speed just until absorbed. Combine the chocolate chunks and nuts in a small bowl and stir into the dough.

4 Using about 1 tablespoon of dough for each cookie, gently shape the dough into balls and drop them about 3 inches apart onto ungreased baking sheets. For perfectly uniform cookies, scoop the dough using a 1 1/2-inch-diameter ice-cream scoop, leveling the dough off across the top before dropping onto the baking sheets. Bake for about 12 minutes, or until the cookies begin to color (you'll have to look carefully). Do not overbake. Let sit for 2 minutes, then transfer to wire racks to cool completely.

Oatmeal CCCs

4 ounces (1 stick) unsalted
  butter, softened

6 tablespoons granulated
  sugar

1/2 cup packed light brown
  sugar

1 teaspoon vanilla extract

1 large egg

1 1/2 cups old-fashioned
  rolled oats

3/4 cup all-purpose flour

1/2 teaspoon baking soda

1/4 teaspoon cinnamon

1 cup semisweet chocolate
  chunks or chips, raisins,
  or chocolate-covered
  raisins

1 cup (3 1/2 ounces) large
  pecan or walnut pieces
  (optional)

About 2 1/2 dozen cookies

Crisp and crunchy, these oatmeal cookies are jammed full of nuts and chocolate. For a classic oatmeal cookie, omit the chips and substitute raisins. Or try adding chocolate-covered raisins. You can always find them at the movie theater.

1. Preheat oven to 350 degrees F.

2. In a medium bowl, using an electric mixer, beat the butter, sugars, and vanilla until well combined. Beat in the egg. Scrape down the bowl using a rubber spatula and beat for a few more seconds. Beat in the oats.

3. In a small bowl, whisk together the flour, baking soda, and cinnamon. Add the dry ingredients to the wet mixture, and mix on low speed just until absorbed. Combine the chocolate chunks (or raisins) and nuts, if desired, in a small bowl and stir them into the dough.

4. Shape the dough into 1 1/2-inch balls and drop them about 3 inches apart onto ungreased baking sheets. For perfectly uniform cookies, scoop the dough using a 1 1/2-inch-diameter ice-cream scoop, leveling the dough off across the top before dropping onto the baking sheets. Use the upper palm of your hand to flatten each ball into a 1/2-inch-thick disk. Bake for about 14 minutes, or until the edges are golden. Let sit for 5 minutes, then transfer to wire racks to cool completely.

Variation: Cranberry-Oatmeal White CCCs

Dried cranberries add a flash of color and tart flavor that offsets the sweetness of the white chocolate in these oatmeal cookies. Follow the instructions for Oatmeal CCCs, but substitute white chocolate chunks for dark chocolate and add dried cranberries. Be sure to use high-quality white chocolate bars (broken in half-inch pieces) rather than white chips, which are too sweet for this cookie. The dried berries should be fresh, moist, and brilliant red.

1 cup white chocolate chunks

1 cup dried cranberries

Twice-Baked Cookies

About Twice-Baked Cookies

If you're a dunker, this is your kind of cookie, whether dipping into milk, sweet wine, or coffee. Many cultures bake a version of this cookie. The Italians make biscotti: **bis** means twice, and **cotti** means cooked. In Tuscany, they dunk biscotti in sweet Vin Santo (Saints' Wine) at the end of a meal. **Mandelbrot,** twice-baked cookies traditionally made with almonds, are essentially Jewish biscotti. Zwieback, those sweet little toasts we gnawed on as teething babies, are baked first as a low loaf of bread, then sliced and baked until they're crisp and dry. **Zwie** means twice; **back** is from the German work for bake.

These are among the easiest cookies to make. Essentially, you mix a dough, form it into a log, and bake it until it's golden. Once the log is baked you slice it into individual pieces, lay them out on the baking sheet, and bake them again to toast the cut edges.

Twice-baked cookies are crisp, crunchy, and sturdy—ideal for mailing. They're sweet without being rich, because they don't contain a lot of fat (butter, oil, or margarine) in proportion to flour. This contributes to their crunchiness and makes them longer-keeping. It also means that the flavor of the other ingredients is accentuated. While it's always important to bake with fresh ingredients, it's especially important here.

We may never know whether it was an Italian **nonna** or a Jewish **bubbie** who first decided to roll sweet dough into a log, bake it, slice it, and bake it again. Perhaps it was one of those bright culinary concepts that made its way from Milan to Minsk. Or maybe it was a serendipitous discovery, occurring simultaneously in different parts of the world, as two grandmothers touched their dough and got a good idea.

Before Twice-Baking Them—Helpful Hints for Making Them

◎ If you don't own a food processor, you can make cookie dough in the same way you'd make pie dough by hand: Whisk the dry ingredients together in a bowl, cut in the butter using a pastry blender, toss in the chunky ingredients (such as nuts, chocolate chunks, cranberries, etc.), and fold in the wet ingredients. Gather the dough together, shape, and bake.

◎ Taste toasted nuts and dried fruits before you add them. If they have no flavor, your cookies won't either.

◎ Keep a ruler on hand to use when forming the logs of dough. The specified length and width of the logs are important. If a log is too long or too wide, for example, the cookies will be small and flat, and will bake too quickly.

◎ A sharp chef's knife with a 7-inch or 8-inch blade is the perfect cutting tool for biscotti. Place the tip of the knife on the cutting surface above the log. Press firmly while the other hand rests on the dull side of the blade to help stabilize and guide the knife.

◎ Unless the recipe specifies otherwise, slice the logs when they're warm, but not hot.

◎ For a more attractive shape, cut the pieces on a slight diagonal rather than straight across.

◎ The second bake is where you can control the final crispness of your cookies. A hint of brown on the underside of the cookie is generally a good indication that it's done. If you prefer cookies that aren't quite so dry, bake them for less time.

Best Biscotti with Some

1 3/4 cups all-purpose flour

1 cup plus 1 teaspoon sugar

1 teaspoon baking powder

1/4 teaspoon salt

2 ounces (1/2 stick) cold
   unsalted butter, cut into
   1/2-inch cubes

2 large eggs

1/2 to 1 1/2 teaspoons vanilla
   extract or other flavoring

1 1/2 cups toasted nuts

About 3 dozen cookies

This is a no-fail, easy-to-do, basic recipe for making hard-to-stop-eating crispy, crunchy, nutty biscotti. Use this basic formula and add whatever nuts and flavorings strike your fancy.

The dough is made in a food processor using a quick and simple process: Whir the dry ingredients to blend, then cut in the cold cubed butter by pulsing the machine, just as you would a pie dough. Pulse the machine to mix in the wet ingredients and nuts. Turn the dough onto the table and form two logs. Bake, slice, and bake again. If you don't own a food processor, you can make the dough in a bowl, using a pastry blender (see page 42).

The butter in the dough is left in small pieces (the size of lentils) to give the finished cookie a lighter, more rustic texture. Recipes that call for creaming the butter with the sugar yield a denser, more even-textured cookie.

Always start with toasted nuts. Taste them first. If they don't have flavor, neither will your cookies. If using a food processor, start with whole nuts and be careful not to overprocess them when you add the wet ingredients; that way you'll have big pieces in the finished cookie.

Below the main recipe are some classy and/or classic nutty variations. If you want to bake a variety of biscotti, cut the recipe in half and make one only log (about 18 pieces) of each type.

1 Preheat oven to 350 degrees F. Line a heavy baking sheet with parchment paper or foil, or lightly grease with butter.

2 In a food processor, combine the flour with 1 cup of the sugar, the baking powder, and salt. Process for a few seconds to blend the dry ingredients. Add the cubed butter and pulse the mixture just until the butter pieces are the size of lentils.

3 In a small bowl, lightly beat the eggs and vanilla. Pour them evenly over the dry ingredients. Pulse the machine a few times to blend. Using a rubber spatula, scrape along the bottom of the bowl. Add the nuts and pulse the machine a few more times, just until the dough is evenly moistened.

4 Turn the dough out onto the table. It may seem dry and crumbly. Using the heel of your hand, briskly and lightly mash the dough with a few quick strokes to moisten any dry spots. Gather it together and gently form into a disk. Using a sharp knife, divide it into two equal parts. Form each piece

Nutty Possibilities

into a 12-inch log. Transfer the logs to the prepared baking sheet and flatten slightly to make a rectangular shape about 2 inches wide. Sprinkle with the remaining teaspoon of sugar.

5. Bake for 30 minutes, or until the logs begin to turn golden. Remove from oven and set aside to cool slightly on the tray, 5 to 10 minutes. Leave the oven on.

6. Using a spatula, transfer the logs to a cutting board. Using a large sharp knife and a quick downward motion, cut each log crosswise on a slight diagonal into 1/2-inch-thick pieces, discarding (or eating) the ends. Arrange the cookies cut side up on the prepared sheet. (If the baking sheet is buttered, wipe off the crumbs but don't grease again.) Bake 7 to 10 minutes, or until the undersides of the cookies show the barest hint of color. Don't overbake. Leave them on the tray to harden and cool completely. Store in an airtight container at room temperature for up to 5 days.

Variation: Pecan Chocolate Chip

1 recipe Best Biscotti, page 44

3/4 teaspoon plus 1/4
    teaspoon cinnamon

1 teaspoon vanilla extract

1 cup (4 ounces) large pecan
    pieces

1 cup (6 ounces) chocolate
    chips

A familiar flavor combination in an unfamiliar form with a dash of cinnamon. You can substitute raisins for all or part of the chips.

1. Mix 3/4 teaspoon of the cinnamon into the food processor with the other dry ingredients, reserving 1 teaspoon of the sugar as directed. Add the butter. Lightly beat the eggs and vanilla. Mix together the pecans and chocolate chips. Process the wet ingredients, pecans, and chips with the flour/butter/cinnamon mixture. Combine the remaining 1/4 teaspoon cinnamon with the remaining teaspoon of sugar. Sprinkle formed logs with the cinnamon sugar.

2. Bake, slice, and bake again as directed.

continued >

Variation: Cashew Coffee

1 3/4 cup (8 ounces) whole roasted cashews, unsalted

1 recipe Best Biscotti, page 44

2 tablespoons plus 2 teaspoons instant coffee crystals (not instant espresso—it's too bitter)

1 teaspoon vanilla extract

As addictive as cashews are, these cookies are even more so. I developed this recipe for an article I wrote with David Rosengarten for **Food & Wine** magazine on pairing dessert wine with sweets. In lieu of milk, he recommends dipping Cashew Coffee Biscotti in a fine cream sherry such as Emilio Lustau.

Cashews break up too quickly in the processor, and I prefer them whole, so rather than adding them to the wet ingredients, gently knead them into the finished dough.

1 To roast the cashews, preheat oven to 350 degrees F and toast on a jelly-roll pan for 10 to 12 minutes, turning them occasionally, until golden. Cool completely.

2 Mix the dry ingredients in the food processor, reserving 1 teaspoon of the sugar as directed. Add the butter. Lightly beat the eggs with the instant coffee and vanilla. Process the wet ingredients with the flour/butter mixture. Turn the dough onto the table and gently knead in the cashews. Sprinkle formed logs with the remaining teaspoon of sugar.

3 Bake, slice, and bake again as directed.

Variation: Hazelnut Anise

1 1/2 cups (8 ounces) toasted hazelnuts (or whole almonds)

1 recipe Best Biscotti, page 44

1 teaspoon anise seed, crushed

1 1/2 teaspoons vanilla extract

This is a classic Italian combo. I confess, I'm not a big fan of anise, but a hint of this aromatic herb heightens the lovely flavor of the hazelnuts. Crushing the seeds releases their flavor: use a mortar and pestle or break them with the flat side of a chef's knife.

1 To toast the hazelnuts, preheat oven to 350 degrees F and roast on a jelly-roll pan for about 15 minutes, until the outer skins crack. Remove from oven and rub in a terry towel to remove the husk. Cool completely.

2 Mix the anise seed into the food processor with the other dry ingredients, reserving 1 teaspoon of the sugar as directed. Add the butter. Lightly beat the eggs and vanilla. Process the wet ingredients and the hazelnuts with the flour/butter/anise mixture. Sprinkle formed logs with the remaining teaspoon sugar.

3 Bake, slice, and bake again as directed.

Chocolatti Biscotti

4 ounces high-quality bittersweet or semisweet
chocolate

1 3/4 cups all-purpose flour

1 cup plus 1 teaspoon sugar

1 teaspoon baking powder

1/4 teaspoon salt

2/3 cup unsweetened cocoa
(preferably Dutch-
process)

4 ounces (1 stick) cold unsalted
butter, cut into 1/2-inch
cubes

2 large eggs, lightly beaten

1/2 teaspoon vanilla extract

1 teaspoon instant coffee

1 cup coarsely chopped
pecans, walnuts, or hazelnuts (optional)

1 cup (6 ounces) chocolate
chunks, broken into 1/2-
inch pieces, or semisweet
chocolate chips

About 3 dozen cookies

Super-saturated with three kinds of chocolate, these biscotti manage to be dense, fudgy, crisp, and crunchy all at once. A little extra butter makes them richer than other biscotti, but they still contain a relatively low proportion of fat compared to other types of cookies.

As with all biscotti, the quality of the ingredients is especially important: Use the best chocolate you can find. For the melted bittersweet chocolate called for in this recipe, purchase high-quality chocolate bars (such as 3-ounce Lindt bars) in a specialty food store. Dutch-processed cocoa, such as Droste, has a darker color and often a better flavor than regular cocoa.

To add nuts to these cookies—they'll taste like Brownie Biscotti—process in the nuts of your choice at the end with the wet ingredients. If you want one nutty and one plain log, gently knead one-half cup of nuts into half the dough once you've divided it.

As with all chocolate cookies, it's difficult to tell when these are fully baked. You won't go wrong if you use an oven thermometer and follow the recipe. Chocolatti Biscotti are delicate when warm; use a spatula to transfer the baked logs and individual slices.

If you don't own a food processor, you can make the dough in a bowl, using a pastry blender (see page 42).

1. Preheat oven to 350 degrees F. Line a heavy baking sheet with parchment paper or foil, or lightly grease with butter.

2. Melt the bittersweet chocolate in the microwave or in a small bowl set over, but not touching, a saucepan of simmering water (see Melting Chocolate, pages 75–76). Set aside to cool.

3. In a food processor, combine the flour, 1 cup of the sugar, the baking powder, salt, and cocoa. Process for a few seconds to blend the dry ingredients. Add the cubed butter and pulse the mixture just until the butter pieces are the size of lentils.

4. In a small bowl, lightly beat the eggs, vanilla, and instant coffee. Pour them evenly over the dry ingredients along with the cooled melted chocolate. (If adding nuts, scatter them over the melted chocolate.) Pulse the machine about 10 times to blend. Using a rubber spatula, scrape along the bottom

of the bowl. Add the chocolate chunks and pulse about five more times, just until the dough is evenly moistened.

5 Turn the dough out onto the table. It may seem dry and crumbly. Using the heel of your hand, briskly and lightly mash the dough to moisten any dry spots. Gather it together and gently form into a disk. Using a sharp knife, divide it into two equal parts. Form each piece into a 12-inch log. Transfer the logs to the prepared baking sheet and flatten slightly to make a rectangular shape no more than 2 inches wide. Sprinkle with the remaining teaspoon of sugar.

6 Bake for 40 minutes, or until the logs spring back when gently touched. Remove from oven and set aside to cool on the tray for 30 minutes. (Being more delicate, they need to be cooler than the other biscotti when sliced.) Leave the oven on.

7 Using a spatula, transfer the logs to a cutting board. Using a sharp knife and a quick downward motion, cut each log crosswise on a slight diagonal into 1/2-inch-thick pieces, discarding (or eating) the ends. Arrange the cookies cut side up on the prepared sheet. (If the baking sheet is buttered, wipe off the crumbs but don't grease again.) Bake for 15 minutes. Leave them on the tray to harden and then transfer to a rack to cool completely. Store in an airtight container at room temperature for up to 4 days.

Thanksgiving Biscotti

1/2 cup yellow stone-ground
   cornmeal

1 1/2 cups all-purpose flour

1 cup plus 1 teaspoon sugar

1 teaspoon baking powder

Pinch of salt

2 ounces (1/2 stick) cold
   unsalted butter, cut into
   1/2-inch cubes

2 large eggs

1 teaspoon vanilla extract

2/3 cup (2 1/2 ounces) dried
   cranberries

About 3 dozen cookies

The Wampanoag Indians of Plymouth Bay certainly did not have biscotti in mind when they introduced the Pilgrims to cornmeal and cranberries. But if they had, these yellow cookies, dotted with red jewel-like cranberries, could have graced the table at the first harvest feast. These biscotti spread more than most. Place the logs at least 6 inches apart on the baking sheet. If you don't own a food processor, you can make the dough in a bowl, using a pastry blender (see page 42).

1 Preheat oven to 350 degrees F. Line a heavy baking sheet with parchment paper or foil, or lightly grease with butter.

2 In a food processor, combine the cornmeal with the flour, 1 cup of the sugar, the baking powder, and salt. Process for a few seconds to blend the dry ingredients. Add the butter and pulse just until mixture has an evenly gritty texture.

3 In a small bowl, lightly beat the eggs and vanilla. Pour them evenly over the dry ingredients. Pulse the machine a few times to blend. Using a rubber spatula, scrape along the bottom of the bowl. Add the cranberries and pulse the machine a few more times, just until the dough begins to clump.

4 Turn the dough out onto the table. Gather it together and gently form into a disk. Using a sharp knife, divide it into two equal parts. On a lightly floured surface, form each piece into a 12-inch log. Transfer the logs to the prepared baking sheet. Sprinkle with the remaining teaspoon of sugar.

5 Bake for 30 minutes, or until the logs begin to turn golden. Remove from oven and set aside to cool slightly on the tray, 5 to 10 minutes. Leave the oven on.

6 Using a spatula, transfer the logs to a cutting board. Using a large sharp knife and a quick downward motion, cut each log crosswise on a slight diagonal into 1/2-inch-thick pieces, discarding (or eating) the ends. Use a spatula to transfer them back to the baking sheet; arrange them cut side up on the prepared sheet. (If the baking sheet is buttered, wipe off the crumbs but don't grease again.) Bake for 12 minutes, or until the undersides of the cookies show the barest hint of color. Don't overbake. Leave them on the baking sheet to harden and cool completely. Store in an airtight container at room temperature for up to 3 days.

Christmas Cantuccini

1 3/4 cups all-purpose flour

1 cup plus 1 teaspoon sugar

1 teaspoon baking powder

1/4 teaspoon salt

2 ounces (1/2 stick) cold
    unsalted butter, cut into
    1/2-inch cubes

2 large eggs

1 teaspoon vanilla extract

1/2 cup (3 ounces) dried
    cranberries

1 1/2 cups shelled raw pista-
    chios (8 ounces)

About 3 dozen cookies

Cantuccini (pronounced "can-too-chee-nee") is the name for the traditional almond biscotti made in Prato, Italy. In this holiday version, bright red dried cranberries and green pistachio nuts replace the traditional almonds, giving these twice-baked cookies a festive color scheme and zingy flavor.

To maintain the brilliant green of the pistachios through the two stages of baking, it is important to begin with unroasted nuts, which are more intense in color. The dough is made in the food processor, so be careful not to overmix the ingredients once the nuts are added, or the pieces will be too small. If you don't own a food processor, you can make the dough in a bowl, using a pastry blender (see page 42).

A friend of a friend, knowing I was a cookie connoisseur, told me about her favorite biscotti recipe, cut from a magazine, which was made with pistachios and cranberries. She said I simply had to try it. The recipe turned out to be this very one, which I had published in **Food & Wine** magazine two years earlier. Good recipes make the rounds.

1 Preheat oven to 350 degrees F. Line a heavy baking sheet with parchment paper or foil, or lightly grease with butter.

2 In a food processor, combine the flour, 1 cup of the sugar, the baking powder, and salt. Process for a few seconds to blend the dry ingredients. Add the cubed butter and pulse the mixture just until the butter pieces are the size of lentils.

3 In a small bowl, lightly beat the eggs and vanilla. Pour them evenly over the dry ingredients, add the dried cranberries, and pulse the machine a few times to blend. Using a rubber spatula, scrape along the bottom of the bowl. Add the pistachios and pulse the machine a few more times, just until the dough is evenly moistened.

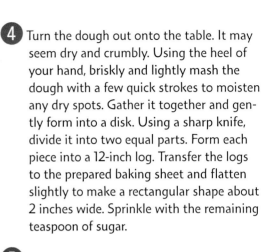

4 Turn the dough out onto the table. It may seem dry and crumbly. Using the heel of your hand, briskly and lightly mash the dough with a few quick strokes to moisten any dry spots. Gather it together and gently form into a disk. Using a sharp knife, divide it into two equal parts. Form each piece into a 12-inch log. Transfer the logs to the prepared baking sheet and flatten slightly to make a rectangular shape about 2 inches wide. Sprinkle with the remaining teaspoon of sugar.

5 Bake for 30 minutes, or until the logs just begin to turn golden. Remove from oven and set aside to cool slightly, 5 to 10 minutes. Leave the oven on.

6 Using a spatula, transfer the logs to a cutting board. Using a large sharp knife and a quick downward motion, cut each log crosswise on a slight diagonal into 1/2-inch-thick pieces, discarding (or eating) the ends. Arrange the cookies cut side up on the prepared sheets. (If the baking sheet is buttered, wipe off the crumbs but don't grease again.) Bake 7 to 10 minutes, or until the cookies show the barest hint of color. Don't overbake. Leave them on the tray to cool completely. Store in an airtight container at room temperature for up to 5 days.

Kitzes Jam Rolls

2 3/4 cups all-purpose flour

1 teaspoon baking powder

1/2 teaspoon salt

4 ounces (1 stick) unsalted

    butter, softened

1 cup plus 2 teaspoons sugar

2 large eggs at room temper-

    ature

1 teaspoon vanilla extract

1 cup apricot and/or raspberry

    jam, or preserves of your

    choice

1/4 teaspoon cinnamon

About 3 dozen cookies

NOTE: Line a heavy baking sheet with parchment paper. This prevents the jam from burning and sticking.

Made with buttery dough, these cookies remain a little cake-like and soft even after the second bake. Jam rolls require one more step than most twice-baked cookies where the dough is formed directly into logs and baked. Here, the dough is first rolled out with a rolling pin, spread with colorful fruit preserves, then folded into a log to bake.

All five of my grandfather Kitzes' sisters were bakers. Although the family owned a teahouse, or **chianyeh** in the Ukraine, my great aunts baked for love, not money. They never wrote down recipes; everything was in their heads (and hands). This recipe came to me from my mother's cousin Sydell, who learned it from her mother—a Kitzes sister.

Stored in an airtight container, these cookies taste better on the second day, and also freeze well, tightly wrapped. For a jewel-like color contrast, roll one log with apricot jam and the other with raspberry; or use any flavor jam you like. I recently made them with my homemade sour cherry jam; they were brilliant both in color and flavor. They are also excellent rolled with a combination of apricot and ginger preserves.

1. Preheat oven to 350 degrees F. To make the dough, in a medium bowl, whisk together the flour, baking powder, and salt. In a large bowl using an electric mixer, cream the butter and 1 cup of the sugar just until combined. Beat in the eggs, one at a time, just until incorporated, and the vanilla; do not overbeat. Scrape down the bowl with a rubber spatula. On lowest speed, or by hand, gradually stir in the dry ingredients.

2. Turn the dough out onto a lightly floured table; it should be soft but not sticky. Form it into a disk and, using a knife, divide it into two equal parts. Roll one piece into a 10-inch log. Transfer the log to a lightly floured piece of waxed paper. Flatten the log into a rectangle, dust the top of the dough, and cover it with another piece of waxed paper.

3. Roll the dough into a 13-by-7-inch rectangle. (Be sure to use a ruler as a guide.) Peel off the top sheet of waxed paper. Using a small palate knife, spread 1/2 cup of the preserves evenly over the dough, leaving a 1/2-inch border all around.

4. Fold the dough in thirds the long way: Beginning with the top edge, use the waxed paper to lift the dough and fold it over. Do the same with the bottom edge to form a three-fold rectangle. Pinch the ends closed.

5 Gently lift the log and transfer it to one side of the prepared baking sheet, positioning it lengthways, seam side down. Repeat the procedure with the remaining piece of dough. In a cup, combine the remaining 2 teaspoons of sugar with the cinnamon. Sprinkle the logs with the cinnamon sugar.

6 Bake the logs for about 40 minutes, or until golden. The logs will spread somewhat and may split down the length as they bake. Place the tray on a wire rack to cool for 10 minutes. Leave the oven on.

7 Using a spatula, transfer the logs to a cutting board. Using a sharp knife and a quick downward motion, cut each log crosswise on a slight diagonal into 1/2-inch-thick pieces, discarding (or eating) the ends. Arrange the cookies cut side up on the baking sheet. Bake for 12 minutes, or until the surface of the cookie feels dry to the touch. Don't overbake. Let cool on the baking sheet for five minutes, then transfer to a wire rack before the jam has a chance to harden. Wrap well and keep at room temperature for up to 2 days, or freeze for up to 2 weeks.

Date Nut Mandelbrot

2 1/2 cups (approximately
9 ounces) walnut halves
and large pieces

2 1/4 cups all-purpose flour

1 1/2 teaspoons baking powder

1/2 teaspoon salt

1 1/2 cups (approximately
10 1/2 ounces) pitted
Medjool or Deglet Nor
dates

2 large eggs

1 1/4 cups plus 1 tablepoon
sugar

3 ounces (3/4 stick) unsalted
butter, melted and cooled

1 teaspoon vanilla extract

1/4 teaspoon cinnamon

About 3 dozen cookies

Mandelbrot means almond bread. It is basically the Eastern European version of Italian biscotti, the only difference being that Mandelbrot is usually made with a little oil rather than butter, so the cookies can be eaten after a meat **or** dairy meal, according to Kosher dietary laws. (Don't ask—it's complicated!) Here, I exchange the oil for an equal amount of melted butter, which has more flavor. But feel free to use 6 table-spoons of vegetable oil instead, if you want authentic, nondairy Mandelbrot.

There are as many ways to flavor Mandelbrot as there are Jewish grandmothers in America; the almonds are frequently replaced by a combination of walnuts, raisins, pecans, and/or chocolate chips.

These twice-baked cookies are jam-packed with walnut halves and moist dates. A portion of the nuts are finely ground and mixed into the flour so that the flavor is absorbed into the dough. If you can't find sticky, sweet Medjool or Deglet Nor dates, substitute bread dates, which are dryer and less flavorful but are available in most supermarkets. Golden and/or dark raisins may also be substituted for the dates, and pecans can take the place of walnuts. This recipe can be halved to make one log yield-ing about 18 cookies.

1. Preheat oven to 350 degrees F. Line a heavy baking sheet with parchment paper or foil, or lightly grease with butter.

2. Using a food processor or large sharp knife, finely chop 1 cup of the walnuts. In a medium bowl, whisk together the flour, baking powder, and salt. Stir in the cup of finely chopped nuts.

3. Cut each date lengthwise and then crosswise into three or four pieces. Toss the dates with the remaining 1 1/2 cups of large walnut pieces.

4. In a medium bowl, beat the eggs and 1 1/4 cups of the sugar with an electric mixer until light in color, about 1 minute. Gradually add the melted, cooled butter and continue to beat until combined. Beat in the vanilla.

5. Using a large rubber spatula or wooden spoon, stir in half the flour/nut mixture. Add the date/nut mixture. Stir in the remaining flour mixture, scraping around the edge of the bowl with a rubber spatula. Turn the dough onto a lightly floured table, pat it into a disk, and using a sharp knife, divide it into two equal parts. On a lightly floured surface, form each piece into

a 12-inch log. Transfer the logs to the prepared baking sheet and flatten slightly to make a rectangle 2 1/2 inches wide. Combine the remaining tablespoon of sugar with the cinnamon and sprinkle over the logs.

6. Bake for 30 minutes, or until the logs are golden. Remove from oven and set aside to cool on the tray, about 20 minutes. (Don't attempt to cut these when they're still warm.) Leave the oven on.

7. Using a spatula, transfer the logs to a cutting board. Using a large sharp knife and a quick downward motion, cut each log crosswise on a slight diagonal into 1/2-inch-thick pieces, discarding (or eating) the ends. Arrange the cookies cut side up on the prepared sheet. (If the baking sheet is buttered, wipe off the crumbs, but don't grease again.) Bake for 15 to 20 minutes or until the undersides of the cookies show the barest hint of color. Don't overbake. Transfer to a rack to cool completely. Store in an airtight container at room temperature for up to 4 days.

Butter Cookies &

About Butter Cookies & Shortbread

Short and sweet—that best describes butter cookies and shortbread. "Short" refers to shortening—in this case, butter. It's the primary ingredient in this family of cookies. The term also refers to the texture of a cookie or pastry made with a high proportion of butter. It's tender, soft, and crumbly. It cuts cleanly and breaks off easily . . . even silently.

The dough is essentially sweetened butter, with just enough flour added to enable it to hold its shape in the oven. Butter cookies and shortbread generally contain no eggs or leaveners. With few ingredients to mask the flavor, the butter in these cookies must be absolutely fresh.

Butter, of course, is churned from the cream that rises to the top of milk when it's fresh from the cow. What's left behind is skimmed milk, which is light and fat-free. A cold glass of skimmed milk is the perfect accompaniment to these rich, buttery cookies. The cookies almost make the cow's milk whole again.

A butter cookie will never attain the crisp snap of a sugar cookie or the luscious chew of a macaroon. It's not wildly textured like a chocolate chip cookie, nor is it showy like a tuile or tulipe. It's a simple cookie composed of the most basic elements of baking: butter, sugar, and flour. The sublime flavor and luxurious texture of butter cookies and shortbread show that greatness can certainly be obtained from humble beginnings.

Guidelines for Baking Butter Cookies & Shortbread

◎ Buy new, unsalted butter before you bake. Even wrapped butter absorbs other flavors in the refrigerator.

◎ Use superfine sugar. It dissolves more quickly into the butter than granulated sugar and gives the finished cookie a finer crumb. Bartenders use this sugar to sweeten drinks. You'll find it in the supermarket sold in 1-pound boxes.

◎ When creaming the butter and sugar, don't overbeat them. They should be soft and blended, but not too fluffy. Incorporating excess air in the mix will cause the cookies to lose their shape more readily in the oven.

Shortbread

◎ Stir in the flour just until it disappears. Overmixing toughens the cookies.

◎ The method with which you combine the ingredients determines the texture of the cookie. Creaming the butter with the sugar results in a smooth, dense cookie. Pulsing all the ingredients together in the food processor, so that the butter is finely granulated, results in a sandy, gritty, coarse-textured cookie. Both techniques make very pleasing cookies.

◎ The dough can be flavored with finely ground nuts, shaved chocolate, spices, or citrus zest. Beware of adding too much texture to the dough—it interrupts the smooth, melt-in-your-mouth sensation of biting into a butter cookie.

◎ There is no need to butter the baking sheets or line them with parchment paper. These cookies have plenty of butter to spare. They won't stick (unless there's jam involved). If you do use parchment paper, the cookies will take a little longer to bake.

◎ Butter cookies and shortbread bake at a lower temperature and take longer to bake than most other cookies. Bake shortbread by color—it's the most accurate way to tell when it's done. The top will be lightly golden when the shortbread is fully baked.

◎ Store different-flavored cookies in separate airtight containers. Butter is a great agent for carrying and transferring flavor and odor. Chocolate shortbread packed with lemon butter cookies, for example, will taste faintly of each other, and neither will taste quite fresh.

◎ These are cool-climate cookies, born in the northern latitudes of Scotland and Scandinavia. In warm weather, refrigerate the baked cookies, well wrapped, if you plan to have them around for a few days. Refrigeration prevents the butter from going rancid and the cookies from becoming soggy. Serve at room temperature.

Variations

To flavor the dough, add the following ingredients:

Utterly Buttery Nutty Shortbread: **1 cup finely ground pecans, walnuts, or hazelnuts**

Lemon Shortbread: **finely grated zest of 2 large lemons and 1/2 teaspoon lemon juice**

Shaved Chocolate Shortbread: **1/4 cup coarsely grated semisweet chocolate** (Use the large holes of a grater to shave the bar of chocolate.)

Ginger: **1/3 cup finely chopped crystallized ginger and 1/2 teaspoon powdered ginger**

Ginger Lemon: **the grated zest of 1 large lemon, along with the crystallized and powdered ginger**

Utterly Buttery Shortbread

8 ounces (2 sticks) unsalted
    butter, softened

2/3 cup superfine sugar

1/4 teaspoon salt

2 teaspoons vanilla extract

2 cups all-purpose flour

Granulated sugar for sprin-
    kling (optional)

About 2 to 3 dozen cookies

This is a beautifully simple yet rich shortbread cookie dough. It has a tender crumb and the perfect level of sweetness. The dough can be rolled out and cut with cookie cutters, pressed into a pan and cut into fingers, or formed into rounds and sliced into wedges.

Shortbread dough couldn't be easier to make: simply blend the butter and sugar, then stir in the flour. With so few ingredients, they must all be at peak flavor. Buy new butter when baking shortbread. Give your flour a whiff; if it's old and rancid, your cookies won't taste fresh.

You can flavor the dough in a number of ways. Add ground nuts, citrus zest, spices, or shaved chocolate after you add the flour. This is not the place for chocolate chunks or large nut pieces. Keep the added ingredients fine-textured and smooth.

1. In a medium bowl, using an electric mixer or by hand using a rubber spatula or wooden spoon, beat the butter, superfine sugar, salt, and vanilla until well combined. Do not overmix; you don't want the butter to become fluffy. Scrape down the bowl using a rubber spatula and beat for a few more seconds. Sift the flour into the bowl and mix on low speed or by hand just until it is absorbed. Scrape the bowl with a rubber spatula and mix again for a few seconds. Stir in any ground nuts or flavorings (see Variations, left). Turn the dough onto the table, gather it together, and knead gently into a smooth mass.

2. The dough can be wrapped in plastic wrap and chilled for up to 2 days, or frozen for up to 2 weeks. Roll the dough into cookies (see page 63) or form it into Pecan Petticoat Shortbread (page 64). When baked and still hot, sprinkle with granulated sugar, if desired.

Utterly

Buttery Cut-Out Cookies

1 recipe Utterly Buttery
    Shortbread, page 61
Granulated sugar for
    sprinkling

About 3 dozen cookies

These rolled-out shortbread cookies are elegant in their simplicity. Made with the basic shortbread recipe on page 61, the dough is rolled out and cut with cookie cutters. If it tears while rolling, simply patch or press the dough back together—it's very forgiving.

Stick to cookie cutters with simple large shapes such as hearts, circles, and legless or thick-legged animals (birds, yes; horses, no). Due to the high butter content, shortbread cookies are not as sturdy as sugar cookies.

Sprinkle the cookies with granulated sugar the moment they come out of the oven. Or, decorate them sparingly with icing and colored sugars for holidays and special occasions (see How to Decorate Cookies, page 130).

1 Make the dough and chill it, covered in plastic wrap, until firm, at least 1 hour or overnight. You can freeze the dough for up to 2 weeks.

2 Preheat oven to 325 degrees F. Divide the dough into 4 quarters and let sit at room temperature, still covered, for about 20 minutes to soften slightly. (If frozen, defrost overnight in the refrigerator.)

3 On a lightly floured surface, gently knead one section of dough with a few quick movements to make it malleable, but not too soft. Flatten it into a patty. On a lightly floured surface, roll the dough to a thickness between 1/8 and 1/4 inch. Run a long metal spatula knife underneath the dough to release it. (Alternatively, roll the dough between two pieces of lightly floured waxed paper or plastic wrap, flipping it once or twice to assure even rolling. Release it from the paper before cutting out shapes.)

4 Cut out shapes with a cookie cutter as close together as possible. Using a palate knife or metal spatula, transfer to ungreased baking sheets, placing them about 1 inch apart. Put the scraps of dough, covered, in the refrigerator to chill. Repeat with the remaining pieces of dough. Press the scraps together, roll them out, and cut. Reroll the scraps, brushing off any excess flour.

5 Bake for about 20 minutes, depending on the thickness of the cookies, or until the edges are golden. For a sugary surface, immediately sprinkle generously with granulated sugar. Let sit for 5 minutes, then transfer to wire racks to cool completely.

Pecan Petticoat Shortbread

1 recipe Utterly Buttery
    Shortbread, page 61
1 cup finely ground toasted
    pecans
Confectioners' sugar for
    stenciling, or granulated
    sugar for sprinkling

16 to 32 wedges

These pie-shaped wedges of shortbread, made from the basic recipe on page 61, are cut from a large round cookie. Before it's cut, the circle is stenciled with powdered sugar through a lacy paper doily. The triangles resemble frilly petticoats.

The addition of pecans makes this shortbread especially tasty. Among one of the softest and sweetest nuts, they meld right into the buttery shortbread dough. Pulse the pecans in a food processor until they're as fine as can be without becoming oily.

In lieu of stenciling the cookie with sugar after it is baked, the dough can be fancifully decorated before it's put in the oven, using tools commonly found in the kitchen gadget drawer. For a simple border, press around the edge of the circle with the tines of a fork. Imprint fun designs with the pointed tips of bottle openers, the blunt end of a chopstick, or the flat side of a vegetable peeler. Sprinkle the cookie generously with granulated sugar while still hot from the oven, then cut into wedges.

1 Preheat oven to 325 degrees F. Lightly butter the inside bottoms of two 8-inch cake pans or springform pans and line with circles of parchment paper. (To make circles, trace the bottoms of the pans on the parchment paper and cut out with scissors.)

2 Make the dough, mixing in the nuts after the flour is added.

3 Form the dough into a round disk and use a knife to divide it in half. Shape the dough into two round patties.

4 Press the dough evenly into the pans. (If pressing decorations into the dough, do so now.) Chill the prepared pans for 15 minutes. Bake for 45 to 50 minutes, until golden brown.

5 Cool the pans on a wire rack for 10 minutes. Run a knife around the edges of the pan to loosen the shortbread. Invert one pan onto a baking sheet, remove the paper, then invert it again onto a wire rack so that it is right side up. Repeat with the second pan. (If using springform pans, simply remove the pan rings and transfer the cookies to a wire rack.)

6 While the disks are still warm but not hot, center a paper doily on one and generously sift confectioners' sugar over it. Lift the doily straight up and shake off the excess sugar. Repeat with the remaining disk. When cool, cut each into wedges.

Sandy Shortbread Fingers

2 cups all-purpose flour

2/3 cup superfine sugar

1/4 teaspoon salt

8 ounces (2 sticks) cold
    unsalted butter, cut into
    1/2-inch cubes

1 teaspoon vanilla extract

3 tablespoons granulated
    sugar, for sprinkling

About 4 dozen rectangles

Gritty, crunchy, buttery, and sweet—I find the texture of these shortbread cookies especially appealing. They may be the quickest and easiest batch of cookies you'll ever bake.

The recipe is almost exactly the same as that of Utterly Buttery Shortbread, but the method of combining the ingredients is completely different. It's a dramatic example of how technique affects the final outcome.

To make, simply whir all the ingredients together in the food processor until powdery. The fluffy mix is then pressed into a baking pan, chilled, baked, and cut into rectangles. To give them a crunchy topping, the cookies are sprinkled with sugar while hot from the oven.

1 In the bowl of a food processor, pulse the flour, superfine sugar, and salt to thoroughly combine. Add the cold butter and vanilla to the flour. Run the machine until the mixture is powdery. Don't let it clump. Press the fluffy mix evenly into an ungreased 13-by-9-inch jelly-roll pan. Be sure the dough isn't thicker in the center of the pan.

2 Chill, covered with plastic wrap, for at least 1 hour or overnight. Preheat oven to 325 degrees F.

3 Bake until the edges are golden brown and the top has a tinge of color, about 35 minutes. Be careful not to overbake. Looks can be deceiving with this one—if the whole top is nicely golden, the cookies are overdone.

4 Remove pan from oven and set on a wire rack. Immediately sprinkle the cookies generously with the granulated sugar. Let them cool for 5 minutes. Using a sharp knife, cut the pan the long way into four equal sections, each measuring 2 1/4 inches. Rotate the pan and cut it into 12 sections across, each a little wider than 1 inch. Using a fork, pierce each piece on the diagonal in three places. Leave the pan on the rack for 20 more minutes. Remove the cookies from the pan using a palate knife or metal spatula and transfer to a wire rack to cool completely.

Jam Buttons

4 ounces (1 stick) unsalted
   butter, softened

1/4 cup superfine sugar

1/8 teaspoon salt

Finely grated zest of 1 orange
   (optional)

1/2 teaspoon vanilla extract

1 large egg yolk

1 cup all-purpose flour

About 2 1/2 tablespoons
   raspberry and/or apricot
   jam

About 32 cookies

Just about the quickest little butter cookie you can make, its soft dough is simply patted into a thick slab and cut out with a small round cookie cutter. The centers of the rounds are indented with your thumb, then spooned with a dollop of jam. Jam Buttons don't even need to be chilled before baking.

These orange-flavored cookies are especially pretty when you use two different jams, such as raspberry and apricot, for a jewel-like variety of colors.

If possible, use a fluted cookie cutter—it gives a flower-like edge to the cookies. You can purchase a set of graduated round cutters in a housewares or baking supply store. It's a handy kit to have for cookie baking and pastry making.

1 Preheat oven to 325 degrees F.

2 In a medium bowl, using an electric mixer or by hand using a rubber spatula or wooden spoon, beat the butter, sugar, salt, orange zest, and vanilla until well combined. Do not overmix; you don't want the butter to become fluffy. Scrape down the bowl using a rubber spatula and beat for a few more seconds. Beat in the yolk. Sift the flour into the bowl and mix on low speed or by hand just until absorbed. Scrape the bowl with a rubber spatula and mix again for a few seconds. Turn the dough onto the table, gather it together, and knead gently into a smooth mass.

3 On a lightly floured surface, press the dough into a 1/2-inch-thick patty. Dip a 1-inch-round cutter into flour and cut out circles, as close together as possible. Gather up the scraps, form a thick patty, and cut out more circles. Continue to do this until the dough is used up.

4 Place the circles on an ungreased baking sheet at least 1 inch apart. Using your thumb or the end of a large wooden spoon, make an impression in the center of each cookie. Stir the jam a little to break it up, then fill each cavity with about 1/4 teaspoon. For variety, fill half the cookies with one flavor jam and half with another.

5 Bake for about 22 minutes, or just until the jam bubbles. Let the cookies cool on the baking sheet for 20 minutes, then transfer them to a wire rack to cool completely.

Thyme Squares

4 ounces (1 stick) unsalted
  butter, softened

1/3 cup superfine sugar

Finely grated zest of 1 large
  lemon

2 teaspoons finely chopped
  fresh thyme, leaves only,
  plus 16 small sprigs for
  decoration

1 cup all-purpose flour

Granulated sugar for
  sprinkling

Sixteen 2-inch squares

The fragrances of lemon and thyme permeate these sweet little shortbread squares. The fresh herb is finely chopped and mixed into the dough, along with grated lemon zest.

Pinch tiny sprigs of thyme from the top of the stems and press them into the center of each square before they're baked. Other herbs, such as rosemary, lavender, or mint, can be substituted for the thyme.

1. Preheat oven to 325 degrees F.

2. In a medium bowl, using an electric mixer or by hand using a rubber spatula or wooden spoon, beat the butter, superfine sugar, and lemon zest until well combined. Do not overmix; you don't want the batter to become fluffy. Scrape down the bowl using a rubber spatula and beat for a few more seconds. Add the chopped thyme. Sift the flour into the bowl and mix on low speed or by hand just until absorbed. Scrape the bowl with a rubber spatula and mix again for a few seconds. Turn the dough onto the table, gather it together, and knead gently into a smooth mass.

3. Flatten the dough and pat it evenly into an ungreased 8-inch-square baking dish. (It helps to place plastic wrap directly on the dough as you pat to prevent your hand from sticking.) Using a sharp knife, score into 16 squares. Place a small sprig of thyme in the center of each square. Cover with plastic wrap and chill until firm, at least 1 hour or overnight.

4. Bake for about 25 minutes, or until the squares turn golden. Immediately sprinkle generously with granulated sugar, then use a knife to cut all the way through along the scored lines. Transfer the baking dish to a wire rack to cool completely. When cool, remove the cookies using a small spatula.

Snow on Chocolate

4 ounces (1 stick) unsalted
    butter, softened

1/2 cup superfine sugar

1/2 cup unsweetened cocoa
    (preferably Dutch-
    process)

3/4 cup all-purpose flour,
    sifted

Confectioners' sugar for
    sprinkling

About eighteen 3-inch
    cookies

Powdered sugar snowflakes are stenciled through doilies onto rich, crunchy, bittersweet chocolate shortbread cookies. The contrast of the lacy white filigree against the dark cookie is striking.

To make the snowflakes, center a small doily directly onto the warm (not hot) baked cookie, sift the sugar over it heavily, then lift the doily straight up to remove it. Shake the excess sugar off the doily and go on to the next cookie. Children love doing this.

The cookie dough can be made with Hershey's cocoa, but a Dutch-process cocoa, such as Droste's, will always be a tad darker and tastier.

If you prefer a snappy chocolate sugar cookie to a softer, buttery one, use Black Beauty dough, page 84, to make Snow on Chocolate cookies.

1. In a medium bowl, using an electric mixer or by hand using a rubber spatula or wooden spoon, beat the butter and superfine sugar until well combined. Do not overmix; you don't want the butter to become fluffy. Scrape down the bowl using a rubber spatula and beat for a few more seconds. Beat in the cocoa. Sift the flour into the bowl and mix on low speed or by hand just until absorbed. (It's very important that the flour be sifted for this recipe.) Scrape the bowl with a rubber spatula and mix again for a few seconds. Turn the dough onto the table, gather it together, and knead gently into a smooth mass.

2. Chill the dough, covered in plastic wrap, until firm, at least 1 hour or overnight. You can freeze the dough for up to 2 weeks.

3. Preheat oven to 325 degrees F. Let the dough sit at room temperature, still covered, about 15 minutes to soften slightly.

4. Divide the dough in half. Gently knead one section of dough with a few quick movements to make it malleable, but not too soft. Press it into a patty. Lightly dust the working surface and the dough with flour. Place a piece of waxed paper or plastic wrap on top of the dough and roll it to a thickness between 1/8 and 1/4 inch. Run a long metal spatula knife underneath the dough to release it once or twice while rolling, then again at the end before cutting the cookies.

Shortbread

5 Using a round fluted cookie cutter measuring about 2 3/4 inches in diameter, cut out circles as close together as possible. Use a palate knife or metal spatula to transfer to ungreased baking sheets, placing them about 1 inch apart. Reroll the scraps until they're all used up. You'll get about 9 or 10 circles. Repeat with the remaining piece of dough.

6 Bake for about 20 minutes, or until the centers spring back when lightly touched. Let the cookies cool on the trays for about 15 minutes, until warm but no longer hot. Center a small doily (a 4-inch doily works well) over a cookie and generously sift confectioners' sugar over it. Lift the doily straight up to remove, shake off the excess sugar, and repeat with the remaining cookies.

7 Transfer the cookies to a wire rack to cool completely. Store in an airtight container for up to 2 days, or freeze for up to a week. Like all shortbread cookies, they will become soggy in humid weather.

Gilded Dark Stars

1 recipe Snow on Chocolate
Shortbread, page 70

Approximately 1 teaspoon
24-karat gold dust

About 2 dozen cookies,
depending on size

Create a glimmering galaxy of stars! Twenty-four-karat gold dust is brushed onto dark, rich chocolate shortbread that has been rolled and stamped out with a variety of different-size celestial-shaped cookie cutters.

Gold dust, which is sifted through a tea strainer, is glitzy, gaudy, and absolutely edible. Be sure to use 24-karat, which is nontoxic and can be found at stores specializing in cake-decorating equipment. Art supply stores often carry 20- or 22-karat gold dust for gilding. These may contain lead and are not safe to ingest.

Gilded shortbread is for dressed-up occasions, such as New Year's and Christmas Eve. It's also lovely cut into heart shapes for Valentine's Day and weddings. Aspic cutter sets, which can be purchased in cake-decorating supply or housewares stores, contain tiny star- and heart-shaped cutters.

If you prefer a snappy chocolate sugar cookie to a softer, buttery one, use Black Beauty dough, page 84, to make Gilded Dark Stars.

1. Follow the instructions for making, chilling, and rolling Snow on Chocolate Shortbread dough. Cut out the dough using a variety of different-size star-shaped cookie cutters. Cut a few crescent moons as well.

2. Using a small tea strainer, sift gold dust over the cookies as lightly or heavily as you like.

3. Bake the cookies following the instructions in Snow on Chocolate Shortbread. Smaller cookies bake more quickly than larger ones. If you've cut out some very small stars, you may need to remove them 5 minutes before the others.

4. Transfer the cookies to a wire rack to cool completely. Store in an airtight container for up to 2 days, or freeze for up to a week. Like all shortbread cookies, they will become soggy in humid weather.

Mostly Chocolate Cookies

About Chocolate Cookies

Chocolate lovers take it any way they can get it—and chocolate cookies are a quick fix. They're portable—you can eat them on the go; and hideable—in case someone else is watching your diet.

Chocolate cookies cry out for milk. Like aged port and Stilton, or Cabernet and prime rib, cold milk and chocolate cookies is a perfect pairing. Whether slugged straight-up from the carton or sipped civilly from a glass, milk enhances the experience of chomping on a chocolate cookie.

It's the quality of the chocolate that determines the difference between a good and a great chocolate cookie. Like the grapes that make fine wine, cocoa beans are affected by where they're grown, how they're grown, and how much care is taken when they're processed into chocolate.

When the fermented cocoa beans are roasted and crushed, much of the fat—or cocoa butter—is pressed out, leaving a dark, thick, bitter slurry called **chocolate liquor** (there is no alcohol involved). Molded and solidified, this paste becomes unsweetened chocolate. When additional cocoa butter is pressed out of the chocolate liquor, the remaining solids are ground into fine powder, which is cocoa.

To make bittersweet or semisweet chocolate, some of the fat is added back into the chocolate liquor along with sugar and vanilla. Milk chocolate is made by adding dry milk solids as well. White chocolate is cocoa butter flavored with sugar, milk solids, and vanilla.

It's cheaper to add fats such as palm kernel oil or cottonseed oil to the chocolate liquor than it is to add back the original cocoa butter. These vegetable fats don't taste as good, because they have a melting point that is higher than our body's temperature, leaving a waxy aftertaste. Cocoa butter melts at 85 degrees F—it melts in your mouth as well as your hand. If chocolate does not contain cocoa butter, it must by law be called confectionery coating or compound chocolate. Fine chocolate is made with cocoa butter. Read labels and taste. Bake with the chocolate you'd most like to eat out of hand.

Bittersweet and semisweet are subjective terms. The bittersweet chocolate made by one company may contain more sugar than the semisweet chocolate made by another. For this reason, it's difficult to specify which to use in a recipe. Either will work—it's a matter of taste. Melted semisweet chocolate chips can also be substituted for semisweet chocolate. Generally, they won't taste as good as the chocolate bars you can buy in 3- or 4-ounce bars made by Lindt, Valrhona,

Guittard, or Ghirardelli. Many gourmet specialty stores now carry high-quality chocolate such as Callebaut, Cocoa Berry, or Peter's that is normally available only in large blocks for commercial use. The stores break the blocks into irregular chunks and sell them by the pound. You'll need a scale at home to weigh out the chocolate when you use a portion to make cookies.

Cocoa powder is naturally acidic. Dutch-process cocoa is treated with a mild alkali that neutralizes it, deepens the color, and mellows the flavor. Droste, a brand of cocoa found in many supermarkets, is Dutch-process. Hershey's, Ghirardelli, and Nestle's cocoa are not alkalized. To determine which you prefer, combine a teaspoon each of cocoa and sugar in a half glass of warm water, tasting at least two brands side by side.

Mayans, the indigenous people of Mexico who first cultivated cocoa beans, referred to chocolate as "food of the gods." Today we tout it as an antidepressant, and even an aphrodisiac. Chocolate is a symbol of indulgence, luxury, and love. Is it any wonder then that chocolate cookies are the most coveted cookies of all?

How to Handle Chocolate

Storing Chocolate   Keep chocolate in a cool, dry place—not in the refrigerator. A dusty white coating on your stored chocolate, called **bloom**, means that some of the cocoa butter has separated and risen to the surface, due to change in temperature. There is nothing wrong with the chocolate except its appearance; it will be fine when melted. Bitter or semisweet chocolate will last at least a year or two when stored properly. Milk and white chocolate have a shorter shelf life, because they contain dairy products. Smell and taste them to determine freshness.

Melting Chocolate   Melting chocolate is not at all difficult, but there are two rules you must abide by: First, the chocolate should not come in contact with any droplets of water—it will seize and lump up. The container you melt it in and the tool you stir it with must be thoroughly dry. Second, chocolate should be melted slowly using low heat. Be vigilant; chocolate burns easily—especially milk and white chocolate. Scorched chocolate is gritty and smells burnt. It can't be salvaged; throw it out and start over.

To Melt Chocolate in a Microwave   Melting chocolate in the microwave is quicker and cleaner than using a double boiler and eliminates the worry of water droplets seizing up the chocolate. When you set the timer, err on the side of caution to prevent burning the chocolate. It's not necessary to fine-chop the chocolate—large pieces are okay. Place the pieces in a dry plastic container or glass bowl and nuke on medium power for 45 seconds. (For melting and tempering up to 6 ounces, a small Pyrex bowl is perfect for the microwave.)

Check the chocolate to see how much is melted by stirring with a rubber spatula—chocolate can fool the eye by retaining its shape even when it is fully melted. If necessary, microwave for another minute or two, depending on how much chocolate there is, until only a few lumps remain. Remove and stir occasionally until the chocolate is smooth and melted.

To Melt Chocolate in a Double Boiler   The amount of chocolate called for in most cookie recipes is too small for a conventional double boiler. To rig up a double boiler for melting 1 to 6 ounces of chocolate, place a small stainless steel bowl over a small pot containing an inch of barely simmering water. Be sure the bowl doesn't touch the water (see Double Boiler, page 12). Chop the chocolate in small even pieces. Place it in the bowl of the double boiler and stir occasionally with a rubber spatula until three-quarters of the chocolate is melted. Remove from heat and stir occasionally until completely melted.

Tempering Chocolate   When chocolate is used as a decoration on cookies, it must be tempered or it will harden with unattractive (but perfectly edible) grayish-white streaks of cocoa butter. Tempering is a process that stabilizes the cocoa butter so that it doesn't separate and float to the surface once the chocolate is cool. Don't be intimidated by tempering. It's simply a process of melting, cooling, and gently stirring the chocolate.

One easy way to temper chocolate for the purpose of decorating cookies is to hold back a third of the chocolate and melt the remainder as described above. Be sure the portion of the chocolate you hold back is finely chopped. Stir the finely chopped chocolate into the melted chocolate. Continue to stir occasionally (and gently) until all the lumps are melted and the chocolate feels cool when touched to a spot just below your lower lip, but is still quite liquid. (The skin below your lip is very sensitive to temperature.) Work quickly once the chocolate is tempered—there is a small window of opportunity here. If the chocolate becomes too cool and hard, it will be difficult to work with.

Brownie Chubettes

6 ounces semisweet choco-
late, chopped

2 ounces unsweetened
chocolate, chopped

3 ounces (3/4 stick) unsalted
butter, cut in pieces

2 eggs

3/4 cup sugar

2 teaspoons instant coffee
crystals

2 teaspoons vanilla extract

1/3 cup all-purpose flour

1/4 teaspoon baking powder

1/4 teaspoon salt

1 cup pecan pieces

1 cup walnut pieces

3/4 cup semisweet chocolate
chips

About 3 dozen 2-inch cookies

These dark, chubby chocolate mounds are essentially freestanding brownies. The texture in the center hovers somewhere between gooey and cakey—the perfect brownie
texture. The cookies even have a cracked, shiny surface, just like a tray of brownies. In
addition, they contain chocolate chips that stay melted and moist for a few hours after
the cookies cool, and they're chock-full of big pecan and walnut pieces. Brownie
Chubettes are best served the day they're made.

For large Brownie Chubs, scoop the cookies with a two-inch ice-cream scoop and
bake them for an extra three or four minutes. You'll get about eighteen cookies.

1 Preheat oven to 325 degrees F. Lightly butter baking sheets or line with
parchment paper.

2 Combine the chopped chocolates and butter in the top of a double boiler
over, but not touching, simmering water, and stir until almost melted.
Remove from heat and stir to melt completely. Set aside to cool. (Alternatively, microwave the ingredients until almost melted, then stir to melt
completely. See Melting Chocolate, pages 75–76.)

3 In a medium bowl, combine the eggs, sugar, instant coffee, and vanilla.
Using an electric mixer on medium speed, beat until the coffee is dissolved
and the mixture thickens, about 1 minute. Using a rubber spatula, stir in the
chocolate mixture. Sift the flour, baking powder, and salt into the bowl and
stir to completely combine. Stir in the nuts and chocolate chips.

4 Drop 1 1/2-inch balls onto the baking sheets, placing them about 2 inches
apart. (An ice-cream scoop measuring 1 1/2 inches in diameter works perfectly.) Bake for about 14 minutes, or until the tops are cracked and the
edges feel firm. The centers will appear a little wet and underdone. Let sit
for 5 minutes, then transfer to wire racks to cool completely.

Choco Lots

6 ounces semisweet or

    bittersweet chocolate

1 tablespoon unsalted butter,

    cut into pieces

1 large egg, room tempera-

    ture

1/3 cup sugar

1/2 teaspoon vanilla extract

2 tablespoons all-purpose

    flour

1/8 teaspoon baking powder

About 20 cookies

Choco Lots are intensely chocolatey cookies. They contain little flour, making them mousse-like and creamy, and are low in sugar for a deep chocolate flavor. They're dark, thin, and soft, with cracked tops.

These cookies are best served the day they're baked. The dough, which is quite easy to make, may be made the day before and chilled.

Because a portion of the chocolate is chopped into small pieces, it's easier to cut up thin bars than thick blocks. Use high-quality chocolate bars, such as Lindt or Valrhona, to make these cookies.

1 Chop or break 4 ounces of the chocolate into pieces. Use a paring knife to cut the remaining 2 ounces into 1/4-inch pieces, the size of chocolate chips. Set aside the small pieces.

2 Melt the 4 ounces of chocolate in the microwave or over a double boiler (see Melting Chocolate, pages 75–76), until a few small pieces remain unmelted. Add the butter and stir to melt completely. Set aside to cool. The mixture will be thick.

3 In a small bowl, using an electric mixer, beat the egg, sugar, and vanilla on medium speed until it thickens, about 1 minute. Stir in the melted chocolate. Sift the flour and baking powder into the bowl and stir to combine. Stir in the small pieces of chocolate. Chill the mixture until firm enough to handle, about 1/2 hour.

4 Preheat oven to 350 degrees F.

5 Roll the dough into about twenty 1-inch balls. Place on ungreased baking sheets about 2 inches apart and flatten slightly with your hands. Bake for about 12 minutes, or until the tops are no longer glossy. Let sit for 5 minutes, then transfer to a rack to cool completely.

Fudge Tops

Silber's Bakery was an institution in Baltimore, where I grew up. As kids, whenever my brother and I accompanied our mother there, we'd wait anxiously for the lady behind the counter to offer us each a Fudge Swirl. They were round butter cookies topped with a thick, dense swirl of dark fudgey icing.

The bakery closed some years ago, and with it went the recipe. So here is my version. The cookies look the same, but the "fudge" is made from a dense chocolate ganache that is piped with a pastry bag; the base is a tender butter cookie.

Ganache, a mixture of heavy cream and chocolate, should be the consistency of very soft butter when it's piped. If it's too stiff, simply heat it briefly, stirring constantly, until it softens. If it's too runny, let it sit at room temperature until it thickens, or chill briefly in the refrigerator, stirring frequently. Once the cookies are topped, the ganache will become firm within an hour or so.

The cookie base will eventually become soft from the ganache. Serve these cookies the day they're made.

1 To make the ganache, in a small pot, scald the cream until bubbles appear around the edge and it's just about to boil. Remove from heat and stir in the chopped chocolate. Stir occasionally until the chocolate is melted and the mixture is smooth and dark. Transfer to a small bowl and set aside to cool until it thickens, stirring occasionally, about 2 hours. The ganache can be made the day before and left covered, at room temperature, overnight.

2 Preheat oven to 325 degrees F.

3 To make the cookies, in a small bowl, using an electric mixer or by hand using a rubber spatula or wooden spoon, beat the butter, sugar, salt, and vanilla until well combined. Do not overmix; you don't want the butter to become fluffy. Scrape down the bowl using a rubber spatula and beat for a few more seconds. Sift the flour into the bowl and mix on low speed or by hand just until absorbed. Scrape the bowl with a rubber spatula and mix again for a few seconds. Turn the dough onto the table, gather it together, and knead gently into a smooth mass. The dough can be made ahead and stored in the refrigerator for up to 2 days.

4 Form the dough into a round patty and quarter into four even pieces. Roll each piece into a log and cut each log into 10 even pieces. Roll each piece into a 3/4-inch ball—about the size of a large marble. Place the balls about 1 1/2 inches apart on ungreased baking sheets and flatten gently and evenly with the heel of your hand so that they're about 1/4 inch thick. Bake for 22 minutes, or until the cookies just begin to color and the bottoms are golden. Let sit for 5 minutes, then transfer to a rack to cool completely.

5 If the ganache was made 2 hours before, it will be soft and moussy. Whisk it a few times to thicken. If the ganache was made earlier in the day or the day before, it will be stiff. Warm it briefly, stirring gently, until it softens a little. Whisk it with one or two quick strokes.

6 Be sure the cookies are completely cool. Place the ganache in a pastry bag fitted with a large star tip (Ateco #5). Holding the bag in a vertical position about 1/2 inch above the cookie, pipe a large dollop of chocolate, leaving a small border of cookie showing around the edge. Repeat with the remaining cookies. The chocolate will firm up in about an hour. To hasten the process, refrigerate the cookies for 5 minutes. Serve at room temperature.

Chocolate Quakes

3 tablespoons unsalted
   butter, melted

1/2 cup granulated sugar

1 large egg

1/2 teaspoon vanilla extract

3 tablespoons unsweetened
   cocoa, preferably Dutch-
   process

1/2 cup all-purpose flour

1/2 teaspoon baking powder

1/8 teaspoon salt

1/4 cup finely ground pecans

1/4 cup semisweet chocolate
   chips

Confectioners' sugar

About 22 cookies

As these cookies spread in the oven, the white, sugar-coated surface breaks apart, revealing the dark cookie beneath. Quakes are deeply chocolate, soft, cakey, and moist. They go into the oven as white balls and come out with boldly graphic black-and-white fissures. They're quite striking on a dessert plate.

These cookies are easy to make. The dark chocolate dough is flavored with finely ground pecans, chilled, formed into balls, and rolled in powdered sugar to form a thick coating. Be sure the nuts are fresh and tasty. To make them even better, toast them for 8 to 10 minutes in a 350-degree oven; then cool completely and grind. You can also substitute walnuts or hazelnuts for the pecans.

1. In a medium bowl using an electric mixer, beat the melted butter, granulated sugar, egg, and vanilla on low speed until pale in color and thickened, about 1 minute. Sift the cocoa, flour, baking powder, and salt into the bowl and mix on low speed until incorporated. Fold in the nuts and chocolate chips. Chill the mixture until firm enough to handle, about 1 hour.

2. Preheat oven to 350 degrees F. Line a baking sheet with parchment paper or foil. Place about 3/4 cup confectioners' sugar in a small bowl (you won't use it all).

3. Form the chilled dough into 1-inch balls and roll each in the confectioners' sugar to coat completely. Place the cookies on the prepared baking sheet about 1 1/2 inches apart. Bake for 12 minutes, or until the cookies are puffed and the sugar has cracked apart. They will appear underdone in the center. Let sit for 5 minutes, then transfer to a wire rack to cool completely.

Black Beauties

2 ounces (1/2 stick) unsalted
　　butter, softened
1 cup sugar
1 large egg, at room tempera-
　　ture
1/2 teaspoon vanilla extract
2/3 cup unsweetened cocoa
　　(preferably Dutch-
　　process)
3/4 cup all-purpose flour
1/8 teaspoon salt

About 3 to 5 dozen cookies,
　　depending on the size

NOTE: To obtain evenly rolled
dough: Rotate and flip the
package occasionally, rolling
it on both sides. Peel off the
waxed paper and reposition
it every so often to prevent
the dough from sticking. Roll
the dough from the center
out.

The beauty of these cookies is in their taste and versatility. Black Beauties are crisp, dark, crunchy, unadorned chocolate cookies with a pleasing bittersweet bite. They make ideal rolled cookies, sandwich cookies, or ice-box cookies.

If you like to keep things simple, bake them plain, pile them on a plate, and pour yourself a tall glass of milk. For a touch of decadence, dip them in melted chocolate or smear them with ice cream on the way to your mouth. (They also make terrific ice cream sandwiches.)

Black Beauties are sturdy enough to decorate with Royal Icing and sprinkles (see How to Decorate Cookies, page 130). For elegant dress-up cookies, apply the techniques for creating Snow on Chocolate (page 70) or Gilded Dark Stars (page 72) to Black Beauty dough. They're also lovely rolled out, cut into circles, and sprinkled with cinnamon-sugar, granulated sugar, or coarse decorating sugar.

For ice-box cookies, the flavored dough is formed into logs, chilled or frozen, then sliced and baked. Flavor the dough with nuts, orange zest, peppermint extract, candied ginger, or spices such as cinnamon and/or pepper.

This dough is used to make Chocolate Mint Marvels, Jammin' Raspberry Peek-a-Boos, and Chocolate Vanilla-Cream Sandwich Cookies.

1 In a stand mixer using the paddle attachment or in a deep bowl using an electric mixer, beat the butter and sugar until light and fluffy, stopping once or twice to scrape down the bowl with a rubber spatula. Add the egg and vanilla and beat to combine. Scrape down the bowl. Sift the cocoa, flour, and salt onto a piece of waxed paper and add half the mixture to the bowl. Mix on low speed until the dry ingredients are absorbed into the dough. Scrape the bowl with a rubber spatula and add the remaining dry ingredients. Mix again until the ingredients are absorbed; the mixture will appear crumbly. Turn the dough onto the table, gather it together, and knead gently into a smooth mass.

2 Cover the dough in plastic wrap and chill for 15 minutes. The dough can be left in the refrigerator for up to 2 days or frozen for up to a week. Let it soften at room temperature before rolling it.

3 To roll and bake the dough, preheat oven to 350 degrees F. Divide the dough into two even pieces. Flatten one section between two pieces of waxed paper or plastic wrap. Roll it out to a thickness of 1/8 inch. The dough must be evenly rolled or some cookies will bake more quickly than others (see Note).

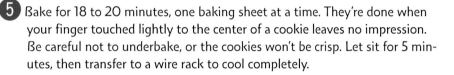 To release the dough from the paper or plastic wrap, peel off the top piece of paper, turn the paper over so the clean side is up, flip the dough onto the clean paper, and peel off what is now the top piece. Cut with cookie cutters, as close together as possible. Peel the cut shapes off the paper and transfer to ungreased baking sheets. Repeat with the remaining piece of dough. Gently knead together the scraps of dough from the two pieces, reroll them, and cut out more shapes. Discard the scraps from that piece.

5 Bake for 18 to 20 minutes, one baking sheet at a time. They're done when your finger touched lightly to the center of a cookie leaves no impression. Be careful not to underbake, or the cookies won't be crisp. Let sit for 5 minutes, then transfer to a wire rack to cool completely.

Chocolate Mint Marvels

1 recipe Black Beauties,
    page 84
2 1/2 teaspoons peppermint
    extract
10 ounces high-quality
    semisweet chocolate
2 ounces high-quality white
    chocolate (optional)
1 teaspoon vegetable oil
    (optional)

About 4 dozen cookies

Girl Scouts will turn green with envy. Crisp, crunchy, peppermint-flavored chocolate cookies are enrobed in dark chocolate—just like the door-to-door version, only better.

To make a dressier version of these classics, drizzle white chocolate over the dark chocolate covering. Use high-quality chocolate to cover the cookies—it makes all the difference.

1 Read the instructions for making, rolling, and baking Black Beauties. Add the peppermint extract to the dough along with the vanilla. Once the dough is made, cover it in plastic wrap and chill for 15 minutes. Preheat oven to 350 degrees F. Divide the dough in half and roll out each piece to a thickness of 1/8 inch. Using a 2-inch-round fluted cookie cutter, cut out circles, as close together as possible. Gather the scraps together, reroll them and cut out more circles. Discard those scraps. Transfer the circles to ungreased baking sheets and bake, one tray at a time, for 20 minutes. Let sit for 5 minutes, then transfer to a wire rack to cool completely.

2 Be sure the cookies are completely cool. Melt and temper the chocolate according to instructions on pages 75–76. Using a small metal spatula, spread a thin layer of tempered chocolate on the bottoms of all the cookies. Chill them in the refrigerator until set, about 10 minutes. Flip the cookies over and spread the tops with the remaining chocolate. Chill until set, about 5 more minutes.

3 To dress up the cookies with white chocolate drizzles, melt the white chocolate in a microwave or double boiler according to the instructions for melting chocolate, pages 75–76. Once melted, stir in a teaspoon of oil to thin the chocolate. Place the cookies close together on the baking sheet and, using a fork dipped in the chocolate, drizzle lines across the surface of the cookies. Chill a few minutes until set. Store in an airtight container for up to 2 days.

Jammin' Raspberry Peek-a-Boos

1 recipe Black Beauties,
    page 84

1/2 to 3/4 cup raspberry jam

Confectioners' sugar for
    dusting

2 to 3 dozen cookies,
    depending on the size
    of the cookie cutter

For some people, chocolate isn't complete without raspberry. Here is a sandwich cookie for those who love this classic combination. The top cookie has a hole in the center so that the raspberry jam peeks through. Once filled, the cookies are dusted with powdered sugar.

For Valentine's Day or Christmas, cut out heart-shaped cookies and make the hole in the top heart using a small round cutter. To make simple round cookies, a cookie cutter kit that contains graduated sizes of fluted round cutters is a handy tool to have.

1 Read the instructions for making, rolling, and baking Black Beauties. Once the dough is made, cover it in plastic wrap and chill for 15 minutes. Preheat oven to 350 degrees F. Divide the dough in half and roll out each piece to a thickness of 1/8 inch. Using a 2- or 3-inch heart-shaped cookie cutter, cut out shapes as close together as possible. Using a small round cutter, about 1/2 to 3/4 inch in diameter, cut a hole from the center of half the cookies before transferring them to the baking sheets. Gather the scraps together, reroll them, and cut out more hearts. Discard those scraps. Transfer the hearts to ungreased baking sheets and bake, one tray at a time, for 20 minutes. Let sit for 5 minutes, then transfer to a wire rack to cool completely.

2 Be sure the cookies are completely cool. Turn the bottom cookies wrong side up. Using a butter knife or small palate knife, spread each cookie with about 1/2 to 3/4 teaspoon of the jam, depending on the size of the cookie. Top with the cut-out cookies, and sift a light dusting of confectioners' sugar over them. Serve the cookies the same day they're assembled.

Chocolate

1 recipe Black Beauties, page 84

2 ounces (1/2 stick) unsalted butter, softened

4 tablespoons shortening

1 1/2 cups confectioners' sugar, sifted

1 1/4 teaspoons vanilla extract

About 30 sandwich cookies

Vanilla-Cream Sandwich Cookies

Vanilla cream icing is sandwiched between dark, crispy chocolate cookies in a home-made version of the store-bought ones you grew up on. Eat them the day they're assembled. These cookies are also terrific eaten cold from the freezer.

1 Read the instructions for making, rolling, and baking Black Beauties. Once the dough is made, cover it in plastic wrap and chill for 15 minutes. Preheat oven to 350 degrees F. Divide the dough in half and roll out each piece to a thickness slightly less than 1/8 inch. Using a 2-inch-round fluted cookie cut-ter, cut out circles, as close together as possible. Gather the scraps together, reroll them and cut out more circles. Discard those scraps. Transfer the cir-cles to ungreased baking sheets and bake, one tray at a time, for 18 min-utes. Let sit for five minutes, then transfer to a wire rack to cool completely.

2 In a medium bowl using a rubber spatula, mash the butter with a rubber spatula until it is evenly softened. Blend in (don't beat) the shortening. Stir in the sifted confectioners' sugar. Add the vanilla.

3 Be sure the cookies are completely cool. Turn half the cookies wrong side up. Using a spoon or pastry bag fitted with a round tip, mound a teaspoon of cream onto the center of each cookie. Top with another cookie and press gently in the center to spread the cream just to the edge. Chill briefly to set the icing, no longer than 10 minutes. Serve the same day the cookies are assembled, or freeze for up to a week.

Tulipes, Tuiles & Lace Cookies

About Tulipes, Tuiles & Lace Cookies

The most marvelous thing about this family of cookies is their flexibility—literally. Made with little flour, the batter spreads out into thin, flat rounds that are malleable and moldable when warm from the oven. They can be formed into cups, cones, coronets, and cigarettes that harden when they cool into lovely vessels for ice cream, fruit, berries, and cream.

Tulipes, tuiles (pronounced "tweels"), and **lace** are dress-up cookies. Not the sort of thing you throw in a lunch box—they'd shatter and break by the time the bus came. These are delicate cookies, meant for nibbling on after a dinner party.

The French make tulipes and tuiles from the same batter we use to make vanilla wafers. Mixed by creaming soft butter and sugar, the batter contains only egg whites and a relatively small amount of flour. Superfine sugar is used because it dissolves more thoroughly into the butter, making a smoother batter and more finely textured cookie.

All the cookies made from this batter are light and crunchy, and will keep for up to a week in an airtight container if the weather is dry. (None of the cookies in this chapter will stay crisp more than a few hours in humid weather.)

Lace cookies are thin, brittle, and riddled with delicate, intricate holes. Held up to the light, they resemble sugary snowflakes. Like the wafer cookies, they can be curled, cupped, or rolled into shape while still warm. Nuts or oats make up the body of these fragile cookies. They usually contain no eggs, little flour, and a high proportion of butter and sugar. Few tools and little skill are required to make these cookies: the ingredients are generally combined in a pot, cooked on the stove top, then plopped by spoonfuls onto the baking sheet.

Common kitchen tools are used to mold the warm pliable cookies. The handle of a wooden spoon is used to form cigarette-shaped cookies. Tuiles are set over rolling pins or the cardboard tube from a roll of paper towels. Tulipes are shaped in soup cups, custard cups, or the mouth of drinking mugs. If a cookie gets too hard and brittle before you have a chance to mold it, simply return it to the oven for a minute or so to soften, then try again.

Sweet and light, tulipes, tuiles, and lace cookies are lovely party cookies. They can be simply arranged on a serving dish with fresh berries scattered about, or presented as edible cups or coronets containing berries and cream, with sauce artfully spilling out onto the dessert plate. Your guests will think you're a master baker.

Nutty Roof Tiles (Tuiles)

1 cup nuts (sliced unblanched
    almonds and/or chopped
    pistachios, pecans, toasted
    hazelnuts, or walnuts)

2 ounces (1/2 stick) unsalted
    butter, softened

1/3 cup plus 2 tablespoons
    superfine sugar

3/4 teaspoon almond extract

1/4 teaspoon vanilla extract

2 large egg whites at room
    temperature

7 tablespoons all-purpose
    flour, sifted

About 28 cookies

Pictured on previous page

NOTE: The quickest way to
measure 7 tablespoons of
flour is to combine 1/4 cup
and 3 tablespoons.

Tuile (French for tile) refers to the curved ceramic roof tiles found throughout the Mediterranean. These thin, crisp white cookies, sprinkled with nuts, are fully baked when a golden rim forms around the edge. While still warm and pliable, they're quickly placed over a rolling pin to harden into a curved shape.

I like to make each batch using a variety of nuts: one quarter cup each of chopped pistachios, pecans, and hazelnuts, and sliced almonds. They look especially pretty with the four alternating colors and textures overlapping on a serving plate.

Be sure the butter is very soft, the sugar is superfine, and the eggs are at room temperature. These all contribute to a finely textured cookie. If you don't want to bother with curling the cookies, leave them flat and transfer them immediately to a cooking rack.

1 Preheat oven to 350 degrees F. In a jelly-roll pan, toast the sliced almonds for about 8 minutes, or until lightly golden. If using other nuts, chop coarsely.

2 Line baking sheets with parchment paper.

3 Be sure the butter is very soft. Using an electric mixer, thoroughly combine the butter and sugar. Beat in the almond and vanilla extracts. Beat the egg whites with a fork just until foamy. Add them gradually and beat until well blended. Sift the flour into the mix and mix on low speed just until combined. Scrape the bowl with a rubber spatula and mix again for a few seconds.

4 Drop a rounded teaspoon of the batter onto the prepared baking sheet and, using a small palate knife, spread the batter evenly into a 3-inch circle. (An ice-cream scoop measuring 1 1/8 inches in diameter also works well.) Place the next spoonful at least 4 inches from the first. Once the tray is covered with circles, sprinkle the center of each circle with 1/2 tablespoon of nuts. Prepare and bake one tray at a time.

5 Bake for about 13 minutes, or until the edges are golden brown. Using a metal spatula, quickly scrape the cookies off the baking sheet, or use your fingers to peel each off the paper, and drape over a rolling pin or the cardboard core of a paper towel roll, until set. (If some of the cookies harden before you get the chance to drape them, put the tray back in the oven for a minute or so to soften them.) Transfer the curved cookies to a wire rack to cool. Repeat the process with the remaining batter on cooled baking sheets. Store in an airtight container for up to 5 days.

Lemon Drop Wafer Thins

4 ounces (1 stick) unsalted
   butter, softened

1/2 cup superfine sugar

Finely grated zest of 2 large
   lemons

2 large egg whites at room
   temperature

1 teaspoon vanilla extract

14 tablespoons all-purpose
   flour, sifted

About 3 dozen wafers

NOTE: The quickest way to
measure 14 tablespoons of
flour is to combine 3/4 cup
and 2 tablespoons.

Like vanilla wafers, these crisp round cookies are fully baked when a golden brown rim forms around the edge. They have a zingy lemon flavor. You can also substitute orange zest for the lemon, or omit the citrus and double the vanilla extract to make a classic vanilla wafer.

Before beginning, make sure the butter and egg are at room temperature. Bake the cookies directly on buttered baking sheets—not on parchment paper, or they won't spread or crisp properly. The wafers become crunchy once they cool.

1 Preheat oven to 375 degrees F. Lightly grease two baking sheets with butter.

2 Be sure the butter is very soft and the egg is not cold. Using an electric mixer, beat the butter, sugar, and lemon zest until thoroughly combined. In a small bowl, beat the egg white with a fork just until foamy. Add it a little at a time and beat the mixture just until well blended, scraping down the bowl with a rubber spatula about halfway through. Add the vanilla. Sift the flour into the mix and mix on low speed just until combined. Scrape the bowl and mix again for a few seconds.

3 Drop rounded teaspoons of the batter onto the prepared baking sheets, about 2 inches apart, or using a pastry bag fitted with a 7/8-inch tip (Ateco #5), pipe out 3/4-inch dollops. For perfectly round cookies, scoop the dough using a 1 1/8-inch-diameter ice-cream scoop, leveling the batter off across the top before dropping it onto the baking sheets.

4 Bake the cookies, one tray at a time, for about 15 minutes, or until the rims are browned. Don't underbake or the cookies will not crisp. Let them cool on the baking sheet for a few minutes, then transfer to a wire rack to cool. They will be crisp when completely cool. In dry weather, store in an airtight container for up to 3 days.

Pecan Praline Lace Cookies, Cups,

1/2 cup plus 2 tablespoons
finely chopped pecans

1/4 cup all-purpose flour

2 ounces (1/2 stick) unsalted
butter, softened

1/4 cup packed dark brown
sugar

1/4 cup light corn syrup

These confections are right on the cusp of cookie and candy.
They have a caramelized brown sugar flavor reminiscent of
Pecan Pralines from New Orleans, but are delicate and lacy.
With little effort, you can make a big splash at your next dinner
party with these fluted dessert bowls, curled coronets, and tasty
cookies.

In the oven, they spread into perfectly flat rounds that can
be molded, while warm, into cups, cones, or cigarettes. The batter is a cinch to make and to mold. Just stir the ingredients on
the stove and spoon the batter onto the baking sheet. You don't
have to spread the batter—it flattens out in the oven. The finished cookies peel easily off the tray.

If using a baking sheet more than once, simply wipe off
the excess butter with a paper towel. Be sure to let the tray cool
before dropping the next batch of batter.

1. Preheat oven to 350 degrees F.

2. In a small bowl, combine the pecans and flour. In a
small saucepan, combine the butter, sugar, and corn
syrup. Bring to a boil. Remove from heat and stir the
dry ingredients into the pan. Transfer the batter to a
bowl and stir occasionally until it thickens into a dough
and is cool enough to handle, about 25 minutes.

3. With moistened hands, roll the dough into various size
balls, depending on whether you're making cookies,
cups, or coronets (see below). Place on ungreased baking sheets, 3 to 7 inches apart, depending on size—
they spread quite a bit. Bake about 12 minutes, or
until the active bubbling subsides. Place the baking
sheet on a rack and let cool until the cookies are firm
enough to lift with a flexible metal spatula but are still
malleable, 3 to 5 minutes. Working quickly, mold each
into shape and set on a wire rack to cool completely. If
the cookies get too cool and brittle to mold, put the
tray back in the oven for a minute to soften.

94

and Coronets

④ Shape and bake the dough.

To make 9 dessert bowls:

With moistened hands, mold each ball using a rounded tablespoon of dough. Place only two balls on the ungreased baking sheet. Have two small soup bowls measuring 4 1/2 to 5 inches across the top ready by the oven. Follow the baking instructions above. When set but still malleable, lift the cookies, one at a time, and place each in a bowl, nutty, bumpy side up. Gently press the bottom to flatten. The sides will ruffle prettily. Wipe the excess butter off the baking sheet and continue with the remaining dough. If you have more than one baking sheet, stagger the baking so that you can mold one tray while the other is in the oven.

Fill with butterscotch ice cream, pumpkin mousse, bananas and cream, or anything that strikes your fancy and goes well with pecans.

continued >

To make 9 ice cream cones:

Follow the baking instructions above for dessert bowls, but when you lift a cookie off the baking sheet, roll it into a cone with the nutty, bumpy side facing out, and hold it for a few seconds to set. Lay it on the cooling rack, seam side down, and place a cylindrical object, such as a pill bottle, in the opening to set until you roll the next cookie.

Fill with scoops of any flavor ice cream or sorbet that complements pecans.

To make 18 dessert coronets:

With moistened hands, mold rounded teaspoons of the dough into balls. Place about nine balls on an ungreased baking sheet. Follow the baking instructions for ice-cream cones; you're making a smaller version of the same. Repeat with a second tray.

Fill with mousse, ice cream, or berries and cream. Place a little dab of cream on the plate to anchor the coronets, and place one or two coronets on each plate with fruit sauce or hot fudge spilling out of the opening.

To make 24 cookies:

With moistened hands, mold level teaspoons of the dough into balls. Place about 12 balls on an ungreased baking sheet. Follow the instructions above. When the cookies are set but still flexible, transfer to a cooling rack. Repeat with a second tray.

To make 24 cigarettes:

Follow the baking instructions for cookies, but when you lift a cookie off the baking sheet, roll it around a chopstick or the handle of a wooden spoon. Lay it on the cooling rack, seam side down. If the cookies get too brittle to mold, put the baking sheet back in the oven for a minute to soften them. To dip the ends in melted chocolate, see pages 75–76 about melting chocolate. Immerse one end of a cookie, then the other, shake off the excess chocolate, and dip the end into a small bowl of grated chocolate.

Lay it on a sheet pan lined with parchment or waxed paper. When all the cookies are dipped, place the tray in the refrigerator for 5 to 10 minutes, just until the chocolate sets.

Oatmeal Lace

2 ounces (1/2 stick) unsalted
butter, softened

6 tablespoons packed light
brown sugar

1 tablespoon milk

1/2 teaspoon vanilla extract

1 tablespoon all-purpose
flour

1/2 cup plus 2 tablespoons
quick-cooking oats

About 20 cookies

These fragile, crunchy cookies resemble miniature doilies of Irish lace. You don't have to be Irish for this harmonious blend of butter, brown sugar, and oats to evoke a kind of nostalgia. When these cookies are served, they disappear fast.

Generally, I prefer the coarse texture of old-fashioned oats in my cookies, but here, quick-cooking oats, which are more finely ground, make a more delicate cookie that is a pleasure to bite into.

1 Preheat oven to 350 degrees F.

2 In a medium bowl, using an electric mixer or by hand, cream the butter and sugar until light and fluffy. Add the milk and vanilla. Stir in the flour, then the oats.

3 Drop rounded teaspoonfuls of dough about 3 inches apart on ungreased baking sheets, or scoop the dough using a 1 1/8-inch-diameter ice-cream scoop, leveling the dough off across the top before dropping it onto the baking sheets. Bake, one tray at a time, for 12 to 14 minutes, or until golden. Place the baking sheet on a rack and cool until the cookies are firm enough to lift with a flexible metal spatula but are still malleable, 3 to 5 minutes. Transfer the cookies to a wire rack to cool completely.

Chocolate Chip Tulipes

5 tablespoons unsalted but-

ter, melted and cooled

4 teaspoons grated

semisweet chocolate

1/2 cup plus 2 tablespoons

all-purpose flour

1 cup confectioners' sugar

Pinch of salt

1/2 teaspoon vanilla extract

3 large egg whites

1 1/2 teaspoons heavy cream

9 dessert bowls

NOTE: If the weather is dry, these cups can be made up to a week ahead and stored in an airtight container in a cool, dry place.

Wafer cookies molded into tulip-shaped bowls are great fun, and rather elegant. Filled with a few scoops of ice cream draped in hot fudge, berries, or cream, they turn a simple dessert into something special. These are dress-up cookies for sit-down dinners.

Tulipes are easy to make, but you must be vigilant at the oven. It's best to make the batter a day ahead and let it set in the refrigerator. Spread the batter in a circle traced on parchment paper, then bake it until golden brown. The soft circle of dough is peeled off, then quickly placed inside a bowl to cool and harden into a fluted dessert cup.

The cookies are speckled with semisweet chocolate that is grated into the batter. For a plain wafer cookie, leave out the chocolate.

Timing is everything in making tulipes. Read this recipe all the way through before starting so you can anticipate each step. To make a fluted cookie bowl that doesn't require spreading the batter, see Pecan Praline Lace Cookies, page 94.

1 In a small pot, melt and cool the butter to room temperature. Using the large holes of a grater, grate the chocolate. (You'll need to grate from a 2-ounce piece of chocolate so you don't scrape your knuckles.)

2 Sift the flour, sugar, and salt into a medium bowl and whisk to combine. In a small bowl, combine the vanilla, egg whites, heavy cream, and butter. Add to the dry ingredients. Using an electric mixer on low speed, beat the ingredients to combine, stopping once to scrape down the bowl. Add the grated chocolate and beat again for a few seconds. Cover the bowl and chill for at least 3 hours or overnight.

3 Preheat oven to 400 degrees F and place a heavy baking sheet in the oven. Have ready by the oven a flexible metal palate knife and a bowl measuring about 4 1/2 inches across the mouth.

4 Trace nine 6 1/2-inch circles on parchment paper using a bowl or lid as a guide. Cut the parchment paper into sections with a circle on each piece. (Don't cut too close to the outline—you'll need a border of paper to grip.)

5 Using a small offset palate knife, spread 2 level tablespoons of batter evenly out to the edges of a circle. Grasp the paper by the border to turn it as you smear the batter. Be sure the center is not thicker than the edges.

6 Place the piece of parchment paper with batter in the oven on the hot tray. Set the timer for 6 minutes. Meanwhile, spread batter onto the next paper circle. As soon it's ready, put it in the oven. This way you stagger the baking and get an assembly line going.

7 Keep a close watch on the oven. The first few cookies can take up to 10 minutes to bake, the last ones as little as 6. When a cookie turns golden brown in the center, grasp the edge of the paper with tongs, remove the paper from the baking sheet, and place it on the counter. Working very quickly, slip the palate knife under the cookie, rotating the paper as you do, to release it. Lift up the circle, center it over the bowl, and push it down, flattening the bottom. The edges of the cookie will flute and wave. Let it set until hard and cool, about 3 minutes. Transfer to a wire rack to cool completely. Repeat with the remaining batter. (If the cookie hardens before you get a chance to shape it, put it back in the oven for a minute or so to soften.)

Macaroons & Meringues

About Macaroons & Meringues

Macaroons and meringues are minimalists: They contain little or no butter, yolks, or flour. Egg white is the basis for these sublime cookies. Billowy snow-white mounds of beaten whites and sugar are gently folded into ground nuts, coconut, or chocolate. Or the whites are stirred, unbeaten, into the ingredients to moisten them into a bakeable batter. Macaroons and meringues are light and crunchy on the outside, often soft and chewy inside, and lower in fat than most cookies.

With few ingredients to buffer the sugar, macaroons and meringues tend to be sweet. Bittersweet chocolate (rather than semisweet), unsweetened coconut (rather than flaked sweetened), nuts, and tart lemon juice offset the sweetness and balance the flavors. While not exactly health food, some macaroons and meringues can be eaten by people who can't digest fat or are allergic to flour. Because they contain no baking powder or soda, they can also be served during Passover, the Jewish holiday that prohibits the use of leavening and flour.

It's hard to tell just by looking that a scruffy coconut macaroon is closely related to a perfectly domed almond "mac." But they're made of the same stuff: egg whites stirred into a base that consists of sugar and coconut or sugar and almonds. It takes no special skill to make spectacular macaroons—just first-rate ingredients and an oven thermometer. (Overbaked macaroons are dry and dull.)

Meringues, on the other hand, must be made by the rules. But the rules are easy and well worth the effort. Meringue is a mixture of egg whites and sugar, beaten until it expands eight-fold into a shiny, sensuous, marshmallow-like mass. Sometimes it's folded into a mixture to lift a cookie in the oven, creating a crisp, cracked crust and hollow chewy center. Other times the meringue is piped or dropped directly onto the baking sheet and dried in the oven at a low temperature to form crunchy little "kisses."

Most meringues and macaroons are a cinch to make. Even the clean-up is easy, with no buttery bowls to wash at the end. The perfect party cookies, there is elegance in their simplicity. But don't wait for a special occasion to serve these delights. You can make up a batch of macaroons in the time it takes to whip an egg white into shape.

Mastering Meringue: The Rules

◎ Cold eggs separate more easily than eggs at room temperature. Be careful not to get any streaks or particles of yolk in the white. The yolk of an egg contains fat, which prevents the white from reaching full volume when beaten. Separate the eggs one by one, dropping each white into a small clean bowl, then transferring it to the mixing bowl. That way, if a yolk breaks, you won't contaminate an entire batch of whites. If only a tiny speck of yolk gets into the white, you can scoop it out with an egg shell.

◎ Let the whites come to room temperature before beating them. Warm egg whites expand more than cold ones.

◎ Keep all utensils clean. Because you want to prevent the egg white from coming into contact with fat, make sure your bowls, rubber spatulas, beaters, pastry bags, and tips are all grease free. Wash them in warm soapy water, rinse thoroughly, and dry. Rub the beaters and the inside of the bowl with a paper towel moistened with white vinegar. Don't use a plastic bowl; it's likely to be coated with residual fat that is hard to remove.

◎ Use an electric mixer if at all possible. Kudos to anyone who tackles meringue-making with a whisk—your arm better be in great shape. A handheld electric mixer will work just fine, but a tabletop mixer (stand mixer) allows you to walk away while the whites are beating, occasionally strolling over to the machine to add more sugar. It also produces the best volume, since it beats strongly and evenly.

◎ Take your time. For optimum volume and stability, start beating the egg whites on slow speed. As they become foamy, increase the speed to medium. Once the egg whites reach soft peak, begin adding the sugar, 1 or 2 tablespoons at a time, waiting at least 10 seconds between additions. Without stopping the mixer, gradually increase the speed to high as you continue adding the sugar. Once the sugar is added, continue beating at high speed for another minute.

◎ Add the salt or cream of tartar once the whites become foamy—not before. Cream of tartar is a white crystalline powdery acid that forms on the inside of wine barrels. It makes beaten egg whites more stable.

Use superfine sugar. It dissolves more quickly and thoroughly into the whites than regular granulated sugar. When a meringue is made with powdered sugar, sift the sugar before adding.

Fold gently. So that you don't deflate the delicate meringue when adding other ingredients, use a large rubber spatula and a gentle scooping motion, rotating the bowl as you work.

To prevent the parchment paper from slipping off the baking sheet when piping meringue from a pastry bag, "glue" a dab of meringue under each corner of the paper.

Meringues are essentially dried, rather than baked. If using more than one baking sheet, it's fine to put both in the oven at the same time, but remember to switch and turn them halfway through.

Don't make meringues on a rainy or humid day. Meringues are hygroscopic; they absorb moisture like a sponge. For the same reason, if you're filling meringue cookies, do so as close to serving time as possible.

Variation: Looney Macaroonies

1 recipe Plain Coconut
    Macaroons, right
1/2 cup chocolate chunks, cut
    into 1/4-inch pieces (or
    use chocolate chips)
1/3 cup coarsely chopped
    banana (from about 1/2
    ripe medium banana)

A tropical combination of three favorite cream pies: chocolate, banana, and coconut—you could go ape for these macaroons. For a chocolate chip macaroon, simply leave out the banana.

Follow the instructions for Plain Coconut Macaroons, gently folding in the small chocolate chunks and banana pieces at the end of the mix. Bake and cool as for Plain Macaroons.

About 2 dozen 2-inch mounds

Coconut Macs :

Plain and Chocolate-Dipped

2 1/2 cups (about 6 3/4
ounces) unsweetened
shredded coconut

2 large egg whites

3 tablespoons hot water

3/4 cup sugar

Pinch of salt

1 tablespoon light corn syrup

1 1/2 teaspoons vanilla
extract

12 ounces bittersweet chocolate (optional)

About nineteen 2-inch mounds

These are the macaroons of your dreams: moist, chewy, and easier than pie to make.

Unsweetened shredded coconut can be found in health food stores. It has a much stronger coconut flavor than the flaked sweetened version (which is full of chemical preservatives) found in supermarkets.

The rounded mounds are formed by scooping the mix with a 1 1/2-inch ice-cream scoop. To make smaller macaroons, dampen your hands and loosely form 1-inch balls.

On the day the macaroons are baked, they have crunchy outsides and soft, chewy insides. Stored overnight in an airtight container, the exterior becomes soft as well—which I prefer.

Chocolate-dipped macaroons are classics. Buy the best bittersweet or semisweet chocolate you can find. You won't use all the chocolate called for in this recipe, but it's easier to dip in deep melted chocolate. The remainder can be reused.

1 Preheat oven to 400 degrees F. Line two baking sheets with parchment paper or aluminum foil. Place the coconut in a large bowl. In a small bowl, beat the egg whites with a fork until foamy.

2 In a small pot, stir together the hot water, sugar, salt, and corn syrup. Using a wet pastry brush, wash down the sides of the pot. Bring the mixture to the boil and remove immediately from heat.

3 Stir the sugar syrup into the coconut. Add the vanilla. Stir in the egg whites until the coconut is evenly moistened.

4 Using a 1 1/2-inch-diameter ice-cream scoop, drop scoops of batter 1 1/2 inches apart onto the prepared baking sheets. Bake for 10 to 12 minutes, just until the coconut begins to turn golden. Remove from oven and cool completely on the baking sheets before removing. Store in an airtight container for up to 2 days.

5 To chocolate-dip the bottoms, make sure the cookies are **completely** cool. Line a baking sheet with foil, or waxed or parchment paper. Temper the chocolate (see page 76) and place in a small bowl. Dip the bottom half of each cookie into the chocolate, scrape off any excess on the side of the bowl, and place on the prepared baking sheet. Once all the cookies are dipped, refrigerate until set and the cookies peel easily off the paper, about 10 minutes.

Chocolate Coconut Macaroons

4 ounces semisweet
    chocolate

2 1/2 cups (about 6 ounces)
    unsweetened shredded
    coconut

1/4 cup unsweetened cocoa
    (preferably Dutch-
    process), sifted

2 large egg whites

3 tablespoons hot water

3/4 cup sugar

Pinch of salt

1 tablespoon light corn syrup

1 1/2 teaspoons vanilla
    extract

About 2 dozen 2-inch mounds

A dark, moist chocolate version of Plain Coconut Macaroons, this recipe is exactly the same, with the addition of cocoa and melted semisweet chocolate.

It's always difficult to tell when chocolate cookies are fully baked—or overbaked. Watch the oven carefully and remove them the moment they can be tilted a little off the baking sheet without falling apart.

If you really want to gild the lily, dip them in chocolate following the instructions for Chocolate-Dipped Coconut Macaroons, page 105.

1 Preheat oven to 400 degrees F. Line a baking sheet with parchment paper or aluminum foil. Melt the chocolate (see pages 75–76) and set aside. In a medium bowl, use your hands to thoroughly combine the coconut and cocoa. In a small bowl, beat the egg whites with a fork until foamy.

2 In a small pot, stir together the hot water, sugar, salt, and corn syrup. Using a wet pastry brush, wash down the sides of the pot. Bring the mixture to the boil and remove from heat.

3 Stir the sugar syrup into the coconut. Add the vanilla, egg whites, and melted chocolate.

4 Using a 1 1/2-inch-diameter ice-cream scoop, drop scoops of batter 1 1/2 inches apart onto the prepared baking sheet. Bake for about 15 minutes, or until the tops are cracked and the macaroons can be tilted a little off the baking sheet without falling apart. Cool completely on the baking sheet before removing. Store in an airtight container for up to 2 days.

Meringue Alphabets

2 large egg whites, at room
temperature

1/8 teaspoon cream of tartar

1/2 cup superfine sugar

Food coloring (optional)

Thirty or forty 3-inch letters

Write messages in meringue by piping letters from a pastry bag fitted with a star tip. The words and letters are fun to use on top of a cake, or to scatter around a dessert buffet. The meringue is simple to make—just follow The Rules on page 102.

You can tint the meringue with a few drops of food coloring. Once it's stiff and shiny, gently fold in the color using a (grease-free) rubber spatula. Supermarket food colors work just fine here. For rainbow lettering, divide the meringue into four small bowls and add a different drop of color to each. Fill the pastry bag with all four colors at once.

An Ateco #2 star tip is a nice size to use—it forms letters that are thick enough to be sturdy, but thin enough to appear delicate. For big, bold letters, use a #5 star tip.

Double or triple the recipe to make more letters.

1. Preheat oven to 200 degrees F. Line two baking sheets with parchment paper or aluminum foil.

2. Place the egg whites in a clean, grease-free bowl of an electric mixer and beat on medium speed until frothy. Add the cream of tartar. Continue to beat on medium high speed until the mixture whitens and soft peaks form. Slowly add the sugar, 1 tablespoon at a time, waiting at least 10 seconds between additions, gradually increasing the speed to high. Once all the sugar is added, beat for another full minute to form a stiff, shiny meringue.

3. To color the icing, use a rubber spatula to gently fold in a few drops of food coloring. "Glue" each corner of the parchment paper to the baking sheet with a dab of meringue.

4. Using a pastry bag fitted with a 1/4-inch star tip (Ateco #2), or a larger star tip for bolder letters, pipe out the characters. If you're printing, pipe them about 1 inch apart. If using script, be sure the letters are joined and there are no thin spots.

5. Bake for 1 hour, then turn off oven and leave the meringues inside to dry until oven is completely cool. Slide a flexible metal palate knife underneath the letters to release them from the paper.

Almond–Pine Nut Macaroons

2 cups (10 ounces) untoasted
pine nuts

8 ounces almond paste

1 cup superfine sugar

2 large egg whites at room
temperature

About 30 cookies

NOTE: For this recipe, the
canned almond paste works
better than the almond paste
that's packaged in 7-ounce
tubes.

Chewy almond macaroons studded with crunchy toasted pine nuts (**pignoli**), these puffy cookies are a standard in Little Italy pastry shops. They're among my favorite cookies.

Almond macaroons are easy to make—just mix the almond paste and sugar, gradually add the egg whites, round the batter into balls, and roll them in pine nuts.

Almond paste, the main ingredient in these cookies, is a pliable mixture of finely ground nuts and sugar. It was first created by the Persians circa A.D. 700. The seafaring Saracens introduced it throughout the Mediterranean, where it became the basis for many confections in southern France, Italy, and Spain.

You can find almond paste in the supermarket; it's sold in 8-ounce cans. Don't confuse it with marzipan, which contains much more sugar.

1. Preheat oven to 325 degrees F. Line two cookie trays with parchment paper or aluminum foil. Spread the pine nuts onto a jelly-roll pan lined with waxed or parchment paper.

2. Break the almond paste into chunks and place in the bowl of a food processor. Add the sugar and process until the mixture is homogenous, stopping once to scrape down the bowl using a rubber spatula. Add the egg whites and process until smooth. Scrape again and process for a few more seconds.

3. The mixture will be sticky, but with a light touch and moist hands it can be gently rolled. Keep a damp towel nearby to wipe and wet your hands. Using damp hands, round the mix into scant 1-inch balls and drop the balls onto the tray of pine nuts. Once you have three or four balls formed, roll them in the nuts to cover completely. Place about 16 balls 1 1/2 inches apart on the prepared baking sheets.

4. Bake the first tray while preparing the second, until the cookies are pale golden and puffy, about 25 minutes. Place the baking sheets on wire cooling racks and cool the cookies completely before lifting them off. Store in an airtight container for up to 2 days, or freeze for up to a week.

Chocolate Marbled Meringue Kisses

2 ounces unsweetened
  chocolate

2 large egg whites, at room
  temperature

1/8 teaspoon cream of tartar

1/2 cup superfine sugar

1/2 teaspoon vanilla extract

1 1/2 teaspoons cornstarch

About 3 dozen cookies

Pictured on page 101

Many people shy away from meringues because they're so sweet. Here, unsweetened chocolate, which is marbled into a stiff meringue, offsets the sugar in these crunchy little kisses. They hang in perfect bittersweet balance. Be sure to use a high-quality unsweetened chocolate.

These cookies are fun to make. Melted chocolate is heavily drizzled onto the surface of the meringue; the marbling happens as you scoop and drop. Once the top layer is scooped away, drizzle more lines of chocolate and keep on scooping.

Before you begin, read Mastering Meringue: The Rules, page 102.

1 Preheat oven to 200 degrees F. Line two baking sheets with parchment paper or aluminum foil. Melt the chocolate (see Melting Chocolate, pages 75–76).

2 In a clean, grease-free bowl of an electric mixer, beat the egg whites on medium speed until frothy. Add the cream of tartar. Continue to beat on medium high speed until the mixture whitens and soft peaks form. Slowly add the sugar, 1 or 2 tablespoons at a time, waiting at least 10 seconds between additions, gradually increasing the speed to high. Add the vanilla and beat for another 3 minutes to form a stiff, shiny meringue. Sift the cornstarch over the meringue and gently fold in, using a rubber spatula.

3 Transfer the meringue to a bowl. Using a rubber spatula, heavily drizzle parallel lines of the melted chocolate over the surface of the meringue. (Resist the urge to marble—that will happen as you scoop and drop.) Using a 1-inch-diameter ice-cream scoop or a teaspoon, scrape across the surface of the mixture, crosswise to the drizzled lines, to get a rounded mound of striped meringue. (Use a second spoon to push the mound onto the prepared baking sheet.) Continue scooping until you need to drizzle more chocolate, dropping the meringues about 1 1/2 inches apart on the baking sheets. Continue to drizzle chocolate and scoop until the meringue is used up. You may not use all the chocolate.

4 Bake for 1 hour, then turn off oven and leave the meringues inside to dry until oven is completely cool. Store in an airtight container for up to 4 days.

Some Classic Cookies

About the Classics

When it comes to cookies, **classic** is a subjective term. One person's classic is another's novelty. My friend Michael C., a cookie maven, was shocked to find that Snickerdoodles weren't included in this book. "They're classic," he tells me. I've never eaten one—I've never even seen one. Michael grew up near Lancaster, Pennsylvania, home of the Amish and Shoo-fly pie. I grew up on Rugulah. To me, that's a classic.

Palmier, or Elephant Ears, on the other hand, were not part of my childhood. They were, though, for kids who grew up in Paris. Now almost every bakery makes these sugary puff-pastry cookies. They've become American classics.

Some cookies attain classic stature by way of the home kitchen, and some by way of the supermarket shelf. Chocolate chip cookies are certainly classic (so much so that they get their own chapter). The least domestic among us have baked or eaten these cookies at home. Chocolate Vanilla-Cream Sandwich Cookies are also classic. There's even a collective ritual attached to the way they're twisted apart and licked.

When we try to qualify or classify sweets, we tread in emotional territory. The sweet treats we ate as children are attached to a primal comfort. The memory of their taste and texture tugs at our heartstrings.

Beloved cookies may have been omitted in this chapter, unfamiliar ones included. Some have even been tweaked a bit for a new spin on a familiar favorite. The classics here are a catch-all (or rather a catch-some) collection. But they've all earned the title.

Pecan Sandies

3/4 cup pecans (3 1/2 ounces)

4 ounces (1 stick) unsalted
   butter, softened

6 tablespoons superfine
   sugar

1 1/2 teaspoons vanilla
   extract

1 cup all-purpose flour

1/2 cup granulated sugar

About 4 dozen cookies

These rich pecan butterballs are coated, warm from the oven, in a crunchy, gritty layer of granulated sugar—hence the "sand" in the name. Among the quickest and easiest cookies to make, Pecan Sandies are wonderful at the end of a meal or on a buffet table with café au lait or a glass of milk. They're also sturdy enough to mail, but package them separately or the sugar will get all over the other cookies.

Pecan Sandies are only as good as the quality of your pecans. Be sure the nuts are absolutely fresh and tasty. Toasting nuts heightens their flavor. If you're toasting two or three cups of nuts, leave them in the oven for about 10 minutes. The toasting time is shorter here because there are so few nuts—they'll toast more quickly. You can also make these cookies with toasted walnuts.

1. Preheat oven to 350 degrees F. In a jelly-roll pan, toast the pecans for about 7 minutes. Let cool completely. Pulse them in the food processor until finely ground, but not oily. Lower the oven temperature to 325 degrees F.

2. In a medium bowl using an electric mixer, cream the butter, superfine sugar, and vanilla until light and fluffy. Scrape down the sides and bottom of the bowl with a rubber spatula. Sift the flour into the mixing bowl and mix on low speed just until absorbed. Scrape the bowl again. Add the nuts and mix just until combined. Turn the dough onto the table, gather it together, and knead gently into a smooth mass.

3. Pinch small pieces off the dough and roll each into a ball measuring a scant inch. To make perfectly even balls quickly, scoop the dough using a 1 1/8-inch ice-cream scoop, leveling it off across the top.

4. Place the balls about 1 1/2 inches apart on ungreased baking sheets. While one tray is baking, prepare the second tray. Bake for about 20 minutes, or until the undersides begin to color. Meanwhile, place the granulated sugar in a small bowl. Let the cookies sit for about 4 minutes. While still warm, toss them, a few at a time, in the sugar bowl to coat completely. Place on racks to cool completely. The excess sugar can be sifted and reused. Store in an airtight container for up to 2 days.

continued >

Variation: Pecan Tea Cakes

1 recipe Pecan Sandy dough, page 113

About 3 dozen cookies

I especially love Pecan Sandies when they're rolled out and cut with a 2-inch round fluted cookie cutter—they're thin and crunchy.

1 Place 1/4 of the dough between lightly floured pieces of waxed paper and roll to a thickness between 1/8 and 1/4 inch. Cut with a 2-inch cookie cutter, as close together as possible. This buttery dough is delicate: to lift the cut cookies off the waxed paper, slide under each with a metal palate knife. Combine and reroll the scraps until all used up. Flat cookies bake a little more quickly than balls—in about 17 minutes. Sugar the cookies when warm.

Variation: Mexican (or Greek) Wedding Cookies

1 recipe Pecan Sandy dough, page 113, substituting finely ground walnuts (or any nut you like) for the pecans

About 1 cup confectioners' sugar

About 4 dozen cookies

Although these powdery white cookies have an international name, they are American classics. The dough is normally sweetened with confectioners' sugar, and the cookies are rolled in more powdered sugar when cool. I find their texture a little chalky. Instead, I use superfine sugar to sweeten the dough. The cookie is crunchy on the inside and powdery sweet on the outside.

1 Follow the instructions for making, forming, and baking Pecan Sandy dough, using walnuts or any nut you prefer. Let the cookies cool completely. Instead of the granulated sugar, place the confectioners' sugar in a bowl and roll them in the sugar to coat. The excess sugar can be sifted and reused. Store in an airtight container for up to 2 days. Just before serving, sift more confectioners' sugar over the cookies.

Crunchy Cranberry Oatmeal Cookies

6 ounces (1 1/2 sticks) unsalted
butter, softened

2/3 cup granulated sugar

2/3 cup packed light brown
sugar

1/4 teaspoon salt

1 teaspoon vanilla

1 large egg

1/2 cup old-fashioned rolled
oats

2/3 cup all-purpose flour

1/2 teaspoon baking soda

2/3 cup dried cranberries

2 cups large pecan pieces

About 3 dozen cookies

NOTE: Be sure to bake these
cookies on parchment paper.
They will spread too much on
a buttered baking sheet.

Craggy, crunchy, lumpy, bumpy, and a little lacy, these delicate oatmeal cookies spread out to thin, crispy edges. In a twist on the classic version, tart dried cranberries are added instead of raisins, to offset the sweetness of the cookie. Don't leave the nuts out of this recipe—they give the cookies their shape. Be sure the pecan pieces are large.

For a more traditional, substantial oatmeal cookie, use the Oatmeal CCC recipe on page 41, omitting the chips and substituting raisins or chocolate-covered raisins.

1 Preheat oven to 350 degrees F. Line baking sheets with parchment paper.

2 In a medium bowl, using an electric mixer, beat the butter, sugars, salt, and vanilla until light and fluffy. Beat in the egg. Scrape down the bowl using a rubber spatula and beat for a few more seconds. Beat in the oats.

3 In a small bowl, whisk together the flour and baking soda. On low speed, add the dry ingredients and mix just until combined. Combine the cranberries and nuts in a small bowl. Stir them into the dough.

4 Shape the dough into 1 1/2-inch balls and drop them about 3 inches apart onto the prepared baking sheets. For perfectly uniform cookies, scoop the dough using a 1 1/2-inch-diameter ice-cream scoop, leveling the dough off across the top before dropping the balls onto the baking sheets. Bake for 12 to 14 minutes, one tray at a time, until the edges are golden brown. The centers will appear slightly underdone. Be careful not to overbake; the cookies will continue to darken on the baking sheets. Let sit for 5 minutes, then transfer to wire racks to cool completely.

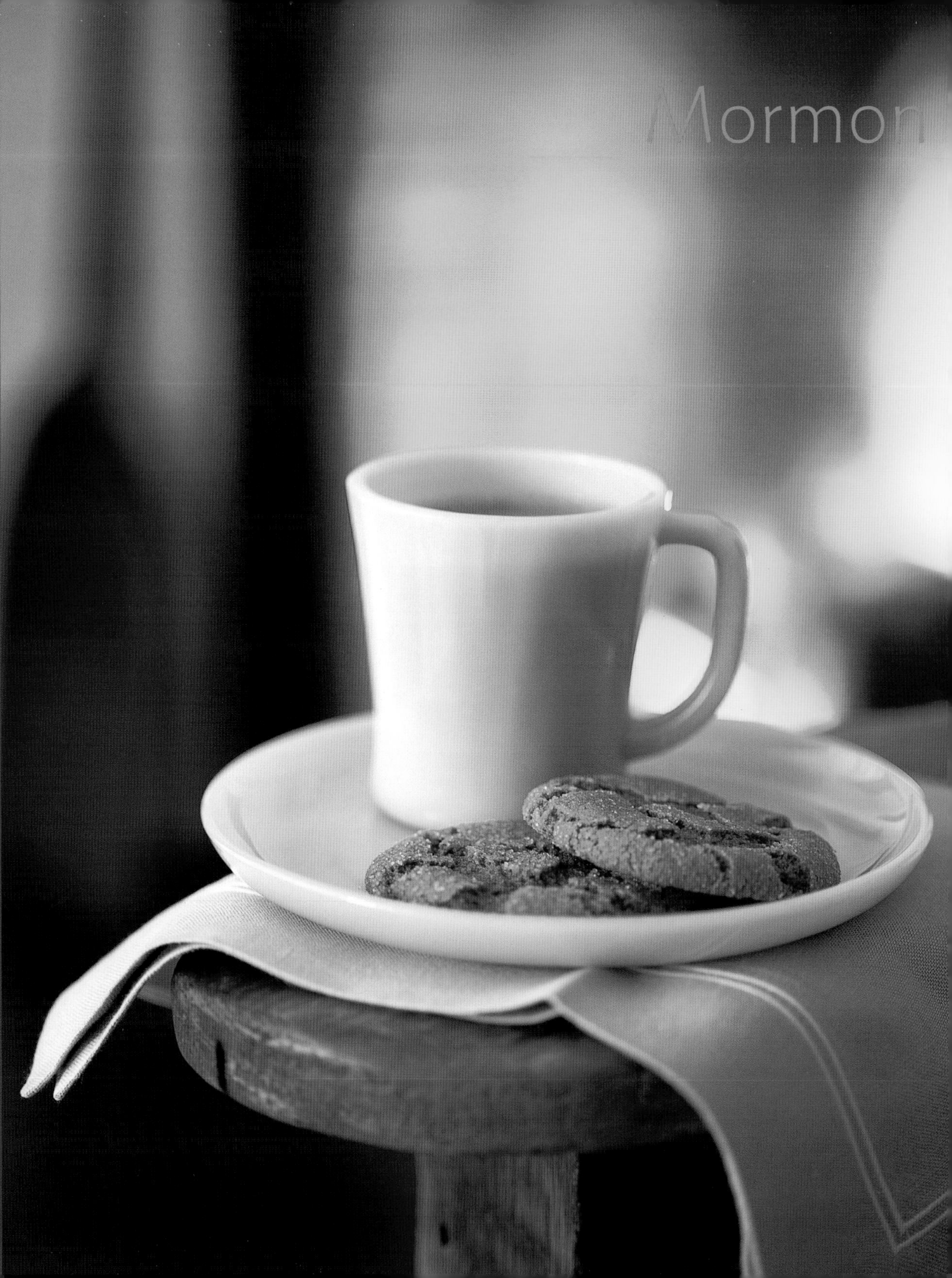

Mormon

Molasses Spice Cookies

6 ounces (1 1/2 sticks) unsalted
   butter, cut in pieces

1/4 cup dark unsulphured
   molasses

1 teaspoon vanilla extract

2 cups all-purpose flour

1 cup plus 1/3 cup sugar

2 teaspoons baking soda

2 teaspoons ginger

2 teaspoons cinnamon

1/4 teaspoon nutmeg

1/4 teaspoon cloves

1/4 teaspoon salt

1 egg, lightly beaten

About 4 dozen cookies

NOTE: For large cookies,
double the size of the balls
and bake a little longer.

My first experience west of the Rockies was as a baker on a cattle ranch in Idaho's Sawtooth Valley. As an avid recipe snoop, it seemed from my New York City perspective that everybody's Mormon mom made a version of this cookie. Whenever I make the cookies east of the Hudson, I'm asked for the recipe.

To my mind, they are the perfect cookies: crispy on the edges, soft and chewy in the center, with a sprinkling of crunchy sugar on top. As they bake, they puff up, heave a sigh, and then collapse as flat as can be. They get that nice cracked top like an old-fashioned ginger snap. Be careful not to overbake these cookies—burnt molasses is bitter.

Being sturdy and long-keeping (if they last, which they don't), Mormon Molasses Spice Cookies are terrific in a lunch box, in the mailbox, or on a winter buffet table. They're excellent dunked in a cold glass of milk.

1   In a medium saucepan, melt the butter over low heat. Remove from the heat and stir in the molasses and vanilla. Set aside to cool.

2   In a medium bowl, sift the flour with 1 cup of the sugar, the baking soda, ginger, cinnamon, nutmeg, cloves, and salt. Whisk to combine.

3   Add the beaten egg to the cooled butter mixture and mix well with a fork. Using a rubber spatula, fold the flour mixture into the butter mixture. Cover the bowl and refrigerate until firm enough to form balls, about 15 minutes. Preheat oven to 375 degrees F.

4   Place the remaining 1/3 cup of sugar in a small bowl. Scoop out walnut-size pieces of the dough and roll into 1-inch balls. Toss the balls in the sugar to coat completely and place on ungreased baking sheets, about 2 inches apart.

5   Bake for 12 to 15 minutes, or until the centers no longer appear raw. (At 12 minutes you'll have soft and chewy cookies; at 15 they'll be crisp.) Let cool on the baking sheet for about 5 minutes, then transfer to wire racks to cool completely. Store in an airtight container for up to 2 days, or freeze for up to 2 weeks.

Black & Whites

4 ounces (1 stick) unsalted
    butter, softened

3/4 cup sugar

1 teaspoon vanilla extract

2 large eggs, at room tem-
    perature

2 large egg yolks, at room
    temperature

1 teaspoon milk

1 cup plus 2 tablespoons cake
    flour

1/2 cup all-purpose flour

1 teaspoon baking powder

1/4 teaspoon salt

Frosting

2 ounces bittersweet
    chocolate

2 3/4 cups confectioners'
    sugar

5 tablespoons boiling water

1/2 teaspoon vanilla extract

About 26 cookies

Also known as Half Moons, these oversize cookies are a New York classic. Even Jerry Seinfeld had something to say about them. In the "babka episode," he sat on the steps of an Upper West Side bakery and pondered the universal question of which side of the cookie to eat first—the chocolate or the vanilla.

Black & Whites are round cake-like cookies, slightly domed in the center, with the flat side frosted half-and-half with vanilla and chocolate icing. Bakeries frost the cookies with **fondant**—a shiny icing that dries hard to the touch. Here, confectioners' sugar frosting is a close facsimile.

The recipe calls for a large percentage of cake flour, which contains less protein than all-purpose flour. Cake flour gives a tender crumb. Be sure not to use **self-rising** cake flour.

1. Preheat oven to 350 degrees F. Line two baking sheets with parchment paper. (Parchment is a must here. Lining the baking sheets with foil or greasing them with butter will cause the cookies to spread too much or unevenly.)

2. In a medium bowl, using an electric mixer, or in a stand mixer using the paddle attachment, beat the butter, sugar, and vanilla until light and fluffy. Scrape the bowl using a rubber spatula. Beat in the eggs and egg yolks one at a time. Scrape down the bowl. Add the milk. In a small bowl, sift the cake flour, all-purpose flour, baking powder, and salt. Whisk to combine. On low speed, add the dry ingredients and mix just until combined. Scrape the bowl and mix again for a few seconds.

3. Scoop the batter using a 1 1/2-inch ice-cream scoop, leveling it off across the top before dropping mounds onto the prepared baking sheets, about 2 inches apart. Place 13 or 14 scoops on each baking sheet. Bake one tray at a time for about 15 minutes, or until the centers spring back when lightly touched. Let sit for 5 minutes, then transfer to wire racks to cool completely. Do not overbake.

4. To make the frosting, melt the chocolate (see Melting Chocolate, pages 75–76).

5. In a medium bowl, use a whisk to combine the confectioners' sugar and boiling water. Add the vanilla. The consistency should be slightly runny, but thick enough to spread. Add more water to thin it or more sugar to thicken it. Using a small palate knife, spread half of the flat side of each cookie with the white frosting. Stir the chocolate into the remaining frosting. You'll most likely need to thin it with more hot water. Spread the remaining halves with the chocolate frosting.

6. If you don't plan to eat the cookies the day they're made, store them un-iced, refrigerated in an airtight container overnight, or freeze them for up to two weeks.

4 ounces (1 stick) unsalted

    butter, softened

1/2 cup granulated sugar

1/2 cup dark brown sugar

1/2 cup creamy peanut butter

1 egg

3/4 teaspoon vanilla extract

1 1/2 cups all-purpose flour

1 teaspoon baking soda

1/4 teaspoon salt

1 cup dry-roasted peanuts,

    chocolate chunks, or

    chocolate-covered

    peanuts (optional)

About 30 cookies

One-third of the acclaimed trio of homemade classic American cookies (which also includes chocolate chip and oatmeal cookies), peanut butter cookies are often dense and clunky. However, these Peanut Butter Crosshatch Cookies are crunchy, light, and airy—the perfect version of this classic.

They are decorated with the traditional fork mark made at right angles on top of the cookie. This crosshatch serves the dual purpose of flattening the dough before it's baked and imprinting the peanut butter cookie with its identifying symbol.

These cookies are wonderful plain, but if you like texture, add dry roasted peanuts, chocolate chunks, or chocolate-covered peanuts. For a chewier Peanut Butter Chocolate Chip Cookie, see page 40.

1 Preheat oven to 350 degrees F.

2 In a large mixing bowl using an electric mixer, beat the butter and sugars until light and fluffy. Beat in the peanut butter. Scrape down the bowl using a rubber spatula and mix again for a few seconds. Beat in the egg and vanilla. Sift the flour, baking soda, and salt onto a piece of waxed or parchment paper and add the mixture to the bowl, mixing on low speed, until the dry ingredients are absorbed. Scrape the bowl and mix again for a few seconds. Add the nuts, chocolate chunks, or chocolate-covered peanuts if you like.

3 Shape the dough into 1 1/2-inch balls and drop them about 3 inches apart onto ungreased baking sheets. For perfectly uniform cookies, scoop the dough using a 1 1/2-inch-diameter ice-cream scoop, leveling the dough off across the top before dropping it onto the baking sheets. Flatten each cookie by pressing a fork into the center in a crisscross pattern—one stroke vertical, the other horizontal. If the fork sticks to the dough, wet the fork.

4 Bake for about 15 minutes, or until the cookies just begin to color. Let sit for 5 minutes, then transfer to wire racks to cool completely. Store in an airtight container for up to 2 days, or freeze for up to a week.

Cookies

Palmier (or Elephant Ears)

1/2 pound frozen puff pastry
(half a package)

3/4 cup sugar

About 2 dozen 2-inch cookies

NOTE: Don't bother trying to scrub the burnt, caked-up sugar on the baking sheets and metal spatula. Simply soak them in warm water—the sugar will melt right off.

You may have seen these light, sweet, crunchy cookies in pastry shops and wondered how they get their shape. The process is easy—puff pastry dough is folded and layered with lots of sugar. Depending on how your imagination works, Palmier resemble either the tops of palm trees or the ears of an elephant.

Puff pastry is light, airy, and full of butter. As the cookie bakes, the sugar between the layers of dough caramelizes to a golden crisp. Don't be put off by the quantity of sugar called for in the recipe. Without it, the cookie tastes quite bland.

These Palmier are made with store-bought frozen puff pastry. (Feel free to make your own if you're ambitious.) It usually comes in 1-pound packages containing two sheets of dough. One sheet will make over two dozen cookies. Try to use dough made with all butter rather than shortening. Read the label. Specialty gourmet food stores often carry high-quality puff pastry.

1 Let the puff pastry defrost in the refrigerator overnight. When ready, take out one sheet of dough. Measure the sugar into a small bowl. Heavily scatter some of the sugar on the table and place the rectangle of dough on it. Coat the top surface of the dough heavily with more sugar. Using a rolling pin, lightly roll the dough out to a height of 10 inches and a width of about 15 inches. Flip the dough once as you roll, adding more sugar as you go. The dough should be about 1/8 inch thick when you finish.

2 Scatter a lot more sugar over the surface of the dough. Fold in the long edges at the top and bottom of the rectangle so they meet in the center. The rectangle will now be about 5 inches tall and 15 inches wide. Heavily sprinkle more sugar over the dough and lightly roll across it to press in the sugar. Fold the top half over to meet the bottom edge. You will end up with a long, thick rectangle measuring about 2 1/2 inches high and about 15 inches wide. Using a sharp knife, cut the rectangle in half. Gently roll over the top and bottom of each piece, being careful not to deform the shape. Press in any remaining sugar as you roll.

3 Place the two pieces of dough on a jelly-roll pan in the freezer for 1/2 hour. Preheat oven to 375 degrees F. Line two baking sheets with parchment paper or foil.

4 Remove one of the pieces of dough from the freezer and, using a sharp knife, slice it every 1/2 inch. Press the sliced edge of each piece into any remaining sugar. Place the pieces, sugar side up, on the prepared baking sheet at least 2 inches apart—the cookies will fan open. (Once the dough is sliced, it can be frozen, tightly wrapped, for up to a week.)

5 While you prepare the second piece of dough, bake the first for about 15 minutes, or until the cookies just **begin** to turn golden. Using a metal spatula, flip each palmier. Bake for another 5 minutes, or until golden brown. Cool the cookies on the baking sheet for 5 minutes, then transfer to racks to cool completely. Meanwhile, bake the remaining tray of cookies.

Rugulah

You don't have to be Jewish to appreciate these rich little rolled-up pastries. They're sold in specialty gourmet food stores and bakeries all over the country. Like bagels, they've become an American classic.

The tender, barely sweetened dough is made with butter and cream cheese. It's rolled out and spread with jam, cinnamon-sugar, nuts, and raisins or chocolate, then formed into small logs or crescents. The contrast of the savory dough with the sweet filling is especially pleasing.

Rugulah are simple to make, freeze well, and are sturdy enough to mail.

4 ounces (1 stick) unsalted butter, softened

4 ounces cream cheese, softened

2 tablespoons sugar

3/4 teaspoon vanilla extract

1 1/4 cups all-purpose flour

Raisin Nut Filling

3 tablespoons apricot jam

5 tablespoons sugar

1 teaspoon cinnamon

1/2 cup golden or dark raisins

2/3 cup coarsely chopped walnuts or pecans

Chocolate Filling

Same as above, but use raspberry or cherry jam instead of apricot

Substitute 3/4 cup semisweet chocolate, finely chopped, for the raisins

2 dozen rugulah

1. In a medium bowl, beat the butter, cream cheese, sugar, and vanilla until smooth. Scrape down the bowl with a rubber spatula and beat for a few more seconds. Add the flour all at once and mix on low speed until absorbed. Scrape the bowl and mix again for a few seconds.

2. Turn the dough onto the table and knead gently into a smooth mass. Divide in half and form each section into a small rectangle. Cover with plastic wrap and chill until firm, at least 2 hours or overnight.

3. To make the filling, place the jam in a small bowl and stir gently with a fork to break it up. In a small bowl, combine the sugar and cinnamon.

4. Remove one piece of dough from the refrigerator and let it sit at room temperature for about 15 minutes, until malleable. Take the second piece of dough out of refrigerator when you're ready to roll the first piece of dough.

5. Heavily flour a piece of waxed paper. Center the dough on it and flour the top of the dough. Place another piece of waxed paper over it. Roll the dough, flipping the whole package once or twice, to form a rectangle measuring 12 inches by 7 inches. End with a long edge of the rectangle closest to you.

6. Using a small palate knife, spread half the jam across the surface of the dough, leaving uncovered a 1/2-inch border along the top edge. Sprinkle the dough with 2 tablespoons of the cinnamon-sugar, half the raisins or chocolate, then half the nuts. Using the flat of your hand, gently press the topping into the dough.

NOTE: You can use 3/4 cup semisweet chocolate chips for the Chocolate Filling. Use the food processor to finely chop them into smaller pieces.

7 Starting with the long edge closest to you, roll the dough away from you, jelly-roll fashion, ending with the seam side down. Roll the waxed paper around the log and chill until firm, about 30 minutes. Repeat with the second piece of dough. Preheat oven to 375 degrees F.

8 Line a baking sheet with parchment paper or foil. Remove the logs from the refrigerator and, using a pastry brush, lightly brush with water. Sprinkle the logs with the remaining 1 tablespoon cinnamon-sugar. Using a sharp knife, trim the edges and slice the logs into 1-inch pieces.

9 Place 1 inch apart, seam side down, on the prepared baking sheet and bake for 25 to 30 minutes, or until golden. Transfer immediately to racks to cool completely. Store in an airtight container at room temperature for up to 2 days, or freeze for up to 2 weeks.

Variation: Crescent-Shaped Rugulah

Same cookie, different shape—with an equal claim to the classic hall of fame.

1 recipe Rugulah

1 Divide the dough in half and roll one piece between two pieces of floured waxed paper into a circle measuring 9 1/2 inches in diameter. Leaving uncovered a 1/2-inch border around the outside edge, smear and sprinkle the toppings, pressing them into the dough gently with your hand.

2 Using a pizza wheel or sharp knife, cut the circle in quarters. Cut each quarter in thirds to get 12 pie-shaped pieces. Starting at the wider edge, roll a triangle towards the point, bending it slightly to form a crescent. Transfer to a tray lined with waxed paper. Continue with the remaining triangles. Repeat with the second piece of dough. Chill until firm, brush lightly with water, sprinkle with the remaining cinnamon-sugar, and bake as described above.

Decorated Cookies

A swipe of colored icing can transform a crisp cookie into an edible work of art. Unadorned, the two rolled-out cookie recipes in this section—sugar and gingerbread—are absolutely delicious. But with just a few simple tools, it's easy to turn these cookies into canvas, and sugar into paint.

Cookie dough is like clay: it can be poked, prodded, and pinched before being baked into decorative forms and whimsical shapes. Once the cookies are baked and cooled, they can be painted, piped, smeared, or sponged with Royal Icing and sprinkled with glittery colored sugars, nonpareils, and metallic dragée.

Some cookies are destined for display rather than the cookie jar. They hang in windows, dangle from mobiles, or are strung from the boughs of a holiday tree. At festive occasions cookies serve as place cards, placards, and party favors. We tend to think of cookie decorating as a children's holiday activity; and it certainly is that. But all ages can be drawn to create fanciful pieces of edible art. Inspiration can come from anywhere—a Jasper Johns exhibit or turning leaves in autumn.

Handling the Dough

While rolling a piece of dough may be the only aspect of cookie-making that requires any skill at all, there is no need to be intimidated by this simple task.

Here are a few tips to help you roll a smooth and even cookie:

Chilling the Dough   Once the dough is made, divide it into even pieces and flatten each piece into a patty about 1/2 inch thick. (If you start with a relatively thin piece of dough, you'll have a head start on rolling.) Wrap each patty separately in plastic wrap and chill for at least 1 hour, or up to 2 days.

Preparing to Roll   It's easiest to roll dough when it is malleable; not too firm and not too soft. Allow chilled dough to soften, still covered, at room temperature, for about 20 minutes. (If the dough is frozen, let it defrost first overnight in the refrigerator.) To speed up the softening process, put the dough in the microwave. Check it after 8 seconds. If it's still rock hard, warm it a few seconds longer. Don't oversoften it.

Rolling the Dough   Dough may be rolled on any flat surface as long as there are no seams or large gouges that could catch the dough. Flour prevents the dough from sticking to the table. A lot of flour will make the job easier, but will change the texture of the cookie. To avoid adding extra flour, roll the dough between two pieces of lightly floured waxed paper (or plastic wrap).

Roll the dough from the center out to the edges. Then roll across the dough in all directions. Rotate and flip the whole package occasionally. Peel off the paper and reposition it every so often to prevent the dough from sticking. Continue to roll until the dough reaches the desired thickness.

Sugar dough, which is not very sticky, can be rolled on a lightly floured surface using just a top sheet of waxed paper or plastic wrap. Scrape underneath the dough occasionally with a long metal palate knife. This releases the dough from the table so that it can be rotated or flipped as you roll (see Tools: Flexible Metal Palate Knives, page 13).

To check if the dough is evenly rolled, peel away the top piece of waxed paper and lightly caress the surface of the dough with the palm of your hand. You'll feel any thick spots. Replace the waxed paper, and roll to even it.

Cutting out Shapes   You must release the dough from the paper before you cut out the shapes, or they'll tear as you try to lift them onto the baking sheet. To release it, peel away the top piece of paper and turn it over with the clean side up. Invert the dough onto the clean waxed paper and peel off what is now the top piece of paper.

If you're rolling without waxed paper or plastic wrap, or using just a top sheet, slide underneath the dough one final time with the long metal palate knife to release it before cutting out the shapes.

Cut out the shapes as close together as possible to avoid creating extra scrap. Some shapes fit nicely into each other; look for places in the dough where an odd shape might fit. In spaces that are too small to fit a full-size cutter, use miniature aspic cutters in shapes such as hearts and stars. These small shapes of dough can be applied to larger ones before the cookies are baked (see Cookie Collage, page 130).

If the cookie cutter sticks to the dough, dip the cutter in flour, tap off any excess, and proceed to cut. Lift the shapes onto the baking sheet using a flexible metal palate knife or spatula.

Snappy Sugar Cookies

3 3/4 cups all-purpose flour

1 teaspoon baking powder

1/2 teaspoon salt

8 ounces (2 sticks) unsalted
butter, softened

1 2/3 cups sugar

2 large eggs, at room temperature

2 teaspoons pure vanilla
extract

About 5 to 6 dozen 3-inch
cookies

NOTE: For a chocolate rolled
cookie that is sturdy enough
to decorate, see Black
Beauties, page 84.

Crisp and sweet with a mild buttery flavor, these simple, sturdy sugar cookies are hard to stop eating. You may intend to nibble just the head off a dinosaur cookie, but before you know it, you've devoured enough bodies to fill Jurassic Park, and guzzled enough milk to float a boat.

1 In a medium bowl, sift the flour, baking powder, and salt. Whisk to evenly combine.

2 In a large bowl, using a handheld mixer, or in the bowl of a stand mixer using the paddle attachment, cream the butter and sugar until light and fluffy, stopping the mixer once or twice to scrape down the bowl with a rubber spatula. Add the eggs, one at a time, beating after each until thoroughly incorporated. Add the vanilla. Scrape the bowl again and mix for a few more seconds. On low speed, add half the dry ingredients. Beat until combined. Add the remaining dry ingredients and beat just until the flour is completely absorbed into the dough.

3 Turn the dough onto the table, gather it together, and knead gently into a smooth mass. Form it into a log and divide into three even parts. Flatten each section into a patty about 1/2 inch thick and cover each with plastic wrap. Chill until firm, at least 2 hours or up to 3 days. The dough may also be frozen for up to a month.

4 Preheat oven to 350 degrees F. Let the dough sit at room temperature, still covered, for about 20 minutes to soften slightly. On a lightly floured surface, roll the dough to slightly more than 1/8 inch thick (see Rolling the Dough, page 126).

5 Cut out shapes with cookie cutters, as close together as possible, and use a palate knife or metal spatula to transfer to ungreased baking sheets, placing them about 1 inch apart. Repeat with the remaining pieces of dough. Press the scraps together, roll them out, and cut, always brushing off any excess flour, until all used up.

6 Bake cookies for about 17 minutes, or until the edges begin to turn golden. Let sit for 5 minutes, then transfer to wire racks to cool completely.

Gingerbread Cookies

3 1/4 cups all-purpose flour

1 tablespoon unsweetened
  cocoa

5 teaspoons powdered ginger

2 teaspoons cinnamon

1/2 teaspoon ground cloves

1/4 teaspoon ground nutmeg

3/4 teaspoon baking soda

1/2 teaspoon salt

6 ounces (1 1/2 sticks) unsalted
  butter, softened

3/4 cup sugar

3/4 cup unsulphured
  molasses

About 4 dozen 3-inch cookies

This rolled-out cookie has a snappy molasses flavor. The dough can be rolled thin for extra-crisp cookies, or thick to construct a gingerbread cottage, castle, or skyscraper. The dough is a little softer than the sugar cookie dough, so handle it gingerly (so to speak).

Because of their chestnut brown color, it's difficult to tell when the cookies are done. When fully baked the edges will darken slightly, and a finger pressed lightly into the center of a cookie will not leave an impression. Gingerbread cookies become crisp once they've cooled completely.

1 In a medium bowl, sift the flour, cocoa, ginger, cinnamon, cloves, nutmeg, baking soda, and salt. Whisk to evenly combine.

2 In a large bowl, using a handheld mixer, or in the bowl of a stand mixer using the paddle attachment, cream the butter and sugar until light and fluffy, stopping to scrape down the bowl with a rubber spatula. Gradually beat in the molasses. Scrape the bowl again with a rubber spatula and mix for a few more seconds. On low speed, add the dry ingredients and mix just until they are absorbed into the dough, stopping once to scrape down the bowl.

3 Turn the dough onto the table, gather it together, and knead gently into a smooth mass. Form it into a log and divide into four even parts. Flatten each section into a patty about 1/2 inch thick and cover each with plastic wrap. Chill until firm, at least 1 hour or up to 3 days. The dough may also be frozen for up to a month.

4 Preheat oven to 350 degrees F. Flour the dough and roll it out between two pieces of waxed paper or plastic wrap to a thickness a little more than 1/8 inch (see Rolling the Dough, page 126).

5 Cut out shapes with cookie cutters, as close together as possible, and use a palate knife or metal spatula to transfer to ungreased baking sheets, placing them about 1 inch apart. Repeat with the remaining pieces of dough. Press the scraps together, roll them out, and cut, brushing off any excess flour.

6 Bake for about 15 minutes, depending on the thickness of the cookie, until a finger pressed gently into the center of a cookie springs back. Let sit for 5 minutes, then transfer to wire racks to cool completely.

How to Decorate Cookies   Some cookies are decorated before they're baked; others are painted with icing once they're cool. A combination of the two methods makes an intriguing cookie. For example, before you put a ginger girl in the oven, squeeze cookie dough hair through a garlic press and attach it to her head; poke indentations for eyes and mouth with the end of a bamboo skewer. Once she's baked and cooled, dress her in polka dot and plaid that is painted and piped on with brightly colored Royal Icing.

Here are some easy techniques for decorating cookies.

Cookie Collage   Larger and more intricate cookies are formed by joining cut-out shapes before they're baked, or placing small shapes on top of larger ones. A line of elephant cookies, for example, parade trunk to tail, in one long cookie. Top a Christmas tree cookie with a small star, or place a little cut-out heart on the chest of a gingerbread man.

Cookie postcards and placards can be made by cutting a rectangular piece of dough to serve as a background, then placing smaller cut-out shapes on top. For a serrated edge, use a fluted pie wheel to cut out the background dough.

To join or collage cookie dough, simply overlap the cut-out shapes; they'll meld in the oven. There's no need to press or adhere them with egg white or water. In the case of joining cookies, be sure there's enough overlap to make a strong connection. Work directly on the baking sheet so that you won't have to transfer the dough.

Tiny aspic cutters, which come in sets containing moons, stars, hearts, and other shapes, can be purchased in cookware or baking supply shops. Once the dough is rolled out and cut with normal-size cookie cutters, use the awkward spaces between those shapes to cut out the smaller ones. You'll have less scrap that way.

Use the contrasting colors of the sugar, gingerbread, and chocolate doughs to highlight shapes within a single cookie. In a line of gingerbread elephants, for example, cut one white elephant from sugar cookie dough. Or make a winter solstice postcard using a background of gingerbread dough. Decorate it with a tree and a crescent moon cut from sugar cookie dough.

Embossing the Dough   Make an impression on the surface of the dough using anything from decorative rubber stamps (the kind found in craft and stationery stores) to common household tools. Bottle openers, vegetable peelers, lemon zesters, and fork tines, to name a few possibilities, can all be pressed into use.

Dip rubber stamps, butter stamps, or cookie stamps (made from glass, porcelain, wood, or clay) into flour, tap off any excess, and press the decoration firmly into the dough. Cut the imprinted pieces out with a paring knife, fluted pie wheel, or cookie cutter.

Use the blunt edge of a paring knife to score lines and patterns in the surface of the dough. This is an easy way to make borders on a postcard or placard. Miniature cookie cutters make sweet impressions: score, rather than cut, the design into the cookie.

The flat end of a bamboo skewer is a good poker for making eyes, mouths, or bellybuttons.

Holes for Hanging   Some cookies are destined for display rather than for the cookie jar. Hang your works of art in windows, suspend them from mobiles, or dangle them from the boughs of a holiday tree. String the cookies with a decorative ribbon or invisible fish line. Use the blunt end of a bamboo skewer or chopstick to punch a hole in the dough once it has been transferred to the baking sheet.

As the cookie expands slightly in the oven, the hole may close. To reopen it, push the implement into the hole and wiggle it a little while the cookie is still hot on the baking sheet.

Cookie Coiffure   Flowing locks of cookie dough hair can be squeezed through a garlic press and placed onto a cookie dough head. Cut the strands short for a beard and moustache.

Cocoa Powder, Gold Dust, and Colored Petal Dust   These edible powders add fuzzy texture or rich sheen. They bond to the surface of a cookie if applied before baking. Use a small strainer to sift them onto the dough, or a small flat-edged brush to dab them on.

Cocoa looks like fur when sifted on the tail of a squirrel or the body of a dog or horse. To cut the bitter taste, whisk a little powdered sugar into the cocoa, being careful not to lighten the color too much.

Gold dust is glitzy, gaudy, and absolutely edible. Be sure to use 24-karat, which is non-toxic and can be found in cake decorating stores. Art supply stores often carry 20- or 22-karat gold dust for gilding. These may contain lead and are not safe to ingest.

Petal dust, which is powdered food color pigment, can be found in a huge array of colors in cake decorating stores.

Any of these powders can also be liquefied with a few drops of vodka or water and painted onto the baked cookie.

Stenciling   Designs that are stenciled onto cookies are crisp, clear, and professional-looking. Small brass and acetate stencils can be purchased in art supply stores, or you can create your own with a mat knife and a sheet of acetate (a strong, flexible, translucent plastic).

A terrific example of stenciled decoration is Snow on Chocolate Shortbread (page 70), where confectioners' sugar is sifted through a doily onto the baked cookie. Powdered sugar is always applied after the cookie is baked; it melts in the oven.

Stained Glass   Sweet panes of "glass," framed by cookie dough, are made with crushed hard candy such as sourballs, lifesavers, or lollipops.

To create stained glass hearts, stars, and other shapes, cut out smaller shapes from larger ones that will serve as frames. Pierce a hole using the blunt tip of a bamboo skewer if you're going to hang the cookies as ornaments.

The dough takes longer to bake than the candy takes to melt in the oven, so bake the cookies first. As they will be returned to the oven later, be careful not to overbake. Leave the oven on.

To make the candy glass, place same-colored candies in plastic baggies; pound with a rolling pin or hammer until finely crushed. Transfer the prebaked cookie frames to a baking sheet lined with parchment paper or lightly brushed with butter.

Fill the open spaces in the cookies with pulverized candy, using the tip of a paring knife to guide and arrange the colors. (For large open areas, heap the candy so that the "glass" will be sturdy.) Rewarm the cookies at 350 degrees F until the candy is liquefied, about 5 minutes. Let cool on the baking sheets. Slide a spatula underneath to release them and store in a cool, dry place.

Royal Icing Cookie Paint

3 large egg whites, at room
 temperature
1 pound (1 box) confectioners'
 sugar

Makes 2 1/2 cups icing to
 cover about 4 to 6 dozen
 3-inch cookies

NOTE: The recipe given above is stiff enough to pipe lines of icing from a pastry bag. To make icing stiff enough to form rose petals, stir in at least 1/3 cup more powdered sugar. For a consistency that spreads so smoothly that a paintbrush leaves no trace of its mark, thin the mix with about 1 or 2 tablespoons of tepid water. These measurements are approximate; adjust according to your preference.

Unlike the frosting on a cake, the icing on a cookie must dry hard so that it can be stacked or packaged. Royal Icing dries to a smooth, opaque, enamel-like finish. The brilliant white icing is an excellent medium for tinting with food color—the pigments come through clear and true.

Royal Icing is actually a meringue made from egg whites and powdered sugar. Depending on how the icing will be used, it can be thinned to a flowing glaze or thickened to a stiff paste by adding water or more powdered sugar.

In addition to its use as an edible paint, Royal Icing is the mortar used to adhere the walls of a gingerbread house. It's quite easy to make using a handheld or stand mixer: simply beat the ingredients until the mixture holds stiff peaks.

To save time and to avoid the remote chance of contamination from raw egg whites, use meringue powder or Royal Icing mix. They require only added water and/or sugar; follow the instructions on the labels. Both mixes can be purchased at a baking supply or cake-decorating store. You can also use pasteurized egg white in place of fresh.

1. In the bowl of a stand mixer fitted with the paddle attachment, or in a bowl using a handheld mixer, begin to beat the egg whites and sugar on low speed. Be sure the bowl and beaters are free of any fat and that there is no egg yolk in the whites. After 30 seconds or so, scrape down the bowl with a rubber spatula and gradually increase the speed of the mixer to medium. Beat until the mixture thickens and stiffens, about 3 minutes.

Decorating with Icing

Once the cookies are baked and cooled, painting, piping, smearing, and sponging colorful icings are some of the most enjoyable ways to decorate cookies.

Storing the Icing   Keep Royal Icing in an airtight container. To prevent a crust from forming while using the icing, keep the container covered with a damp towel or plastic wrap. Royal Icing will keep in the refrigerator for up to 2 days (or up to 5 days if made from a mix). Before reusing, lightly rebeat with a whisk or fork.

About Food Colors   An exciting array of food-grade colors ranging from delicate pastels to brilliant primary pigments are available in liquid, powder, paste, or gel (see page 25). The **liquid colors** sold in supermarkets are the most readily available and work quite well, but offer a limited range of colors: red, yellow, blue, and green. (Orange and purple can also be made by mixing colors.) Liquid colors used by professionals are highly concentrated and come in a wider range of hues. They are packaged in squeeze bottles with twist tops that regulate the flow of color, drop by drop. There's a minimal amount of mess involved. Don't confuse them with liquid airbrush colors that are sprayed onto icing through a gun, and are less concentrated.

Until recently, **paste colors,** which come in small jars of highly concentrated pigment, were probably the most popular food color medium among decorating professionals. I don't recommend them, as they're messy and difficult to use. A small amount of paste is transferred to the icing with a toothpick or bamboo skewer. The thick paste doesn't combine easily with the fluid icing. Also, some pigments have a tendency to dry out. Food paste colors are intense; use them sparingly. They come in a large assortment of colors.

My favorite medium, and relatively new on the market, is **soft gel paste**—a viscous mixture that, like liquid color, is sold in squeeze bottles with caps that regulate the flow, drop by drop. They are easy to use and come in a beautiful range of brilliant and off-beat colors such as teal, mauve, and terracotta.

The fine, colored powder used to highlight pastillage flowers that decorate wedding cakes is **petal dust**. Normally, it's dry-dusted onto the finished ornament. However, when combined with a wet medium such as Royal Icing, the pigment dissolves and colors the icing. Petal dust comes in lovely, unusual shades of color such as moss green and plum. It's easy to use: simply sprinkle it into the icing and stir. The only drawback is that it can take a while for all the powder to dissolve, making it difficult to know how much powder to add initially. Let the colored icing sit a few minutes and stir again before adding more pigment.

Coloring the Icing   Put on an apron and roll up your sleeves. It's not a bad idea to use surgical gloves, which can be purchased in a drugstore, to prevent your hands from staining. Thicken or thin the icing according to how it will be applied.

Divide the icing into as many cups or bowls as you have colors. Pyrex bowls or round plastic containers with lids work well. Leave some icing uncolored; white comes in handy for snow, and for correcting overly intense-colored icing.

Stir the food color into the icing using a small rubber spatula. Scrape down the sides of the bowl and cover with plastic wrap or a damp cloth to prevent a crust from forming.

The intensity of a color is controlled by the amount of pigment used. Proceed with restraint. It's easier to darken than lighten a color. If you accidentally make an icing too intense, remove some and stir in white icing.

Glitz and Glitter: Colored Sugar, Dragées & Nonpareils   A spray of sweet, brightly colored sugar adds glimmer and glamour to a cookie. To get the full impact of their color and sparkle, sprinkle colored sugar crystals, **dragées**, and nonpareils onto the iced cookies while the Royal Icing is still wet. (They can also be sprinkled onto the dough before the cookies are baked, but the colors will be more muted and they won't adhere as well.)

Coarse, colored sugars can be purchased in the supermarket or in a cake-decorating shop. You can make your own by rubbing powder or liquid food color into sugar.

Nonpareils, those tiny beads on top of round chocolates, come in a rainbow of colors. Silver, gold, and multicolored **dragées**, the shiny, hard, metallic balls that often adorn holiday cookies, come in a range of sizes; they can be as tiny as nonpareils or as large as BB gun ammunition. Take care not to get them wet—the metallic coating will melt off.

How to Apply Icing and Sprinkles   Of all the ways to apply the icing, the most fun is to brush it on with a paintbrush; inexpensive children's brushes work just fine. To prevent mixing the colors, use different brushes or keep a water glass and towel nearby to swoosh and wipe, just as when painting with watercolor.

The background color is applied with a flat brush. Details such as stripes, squiggles, and dots can be painted right over the wet background icing using a round-tip brush. For example, purple dots or stripes on a butterfly wing can be painted onto a background color of yellow. The surface of the icing will dry smooth, flat, and glossy.

For a feathered effect, draw the detail lines out with the point of a toothpick.

A pastry bag fitted with a round writing tip can also be used to pipe outlines and fine details.

Use a small piece of natural sponge to dab white icing onto a dry background color to create a speckled surface.

Sprinkle colored sugars, nonpareils, and **dragées** over the wet icing. For depth, use two different shades of the same color. For example, paint a cookie leaf with bright green icing, and sprinkle it with dark green sugar crystals.

Royal Icing takes anywhere from ten minutes to three hours to harden, depending on how much extra water is added, how thickly the icing is applied, and the humidity in the atmosphere.

Kids and Cookie Decorating   Kids love making art—and they love to eat sweets. Cookie decorating is the ideal edible art form for children. There's no need to limit cookie decorating to the season of snowflakes and Santa. Organize a birthday or Halloween party around cookie decorating, or get cozy in the kitchen with your own children for an afternoon of baking and art.

Here are some organizational tips to keep the chaos at bay:

◎ Adults willing, children like to participate in every aspect of the process, from making the dough, to rolling and baking the cookies, to painting them with icing. If you're baking with your own children, the activity can take place over a two-day period: make and bake the dough one day; decorate cookies the next.

◎ To make a party for a larger group of children, start with prebaked cookies. Allowing for breakage, figure on about ten cookies per kid, per hour. An hour to an hour and a half is about as long as most kids will stay engaged.

◎ Thin the icing so that it spreads easily with a paintbrush. Fill six or seven bowls (preferably see-through Pyrex) with about 1/2 cup each of brightly colored icings, including white.

Fill small bowls or a muffin tin with an assortment of colored sprinkles. You need only about 1/4 cup of each topping.

Small children like to finger-paint on cookies; older ones prefer to brush on the icing. Using an assortment of flat and round brushes, put at least two brushes in each bowl of colored icing. To avoid mixing colors, remind kids to switch brushes when they switch colors.

Arrange the bowls of colored icings, glittery sugars, and baked cookies within easy reach of the kids. Make a "decorating station" for every six kids to share. A station consists of six or seven colored icings and a muffin tin filled with toppings. If there are more children, repeat the setup so the kids don't have to reach too far or wait for colors.

Roll up sleeves, tie on aprons, and give each child a damp kitchen towel for frequent hand wiping.

Demonstrate for the children how to paint: apply a glob of icing onto a cookie using a flat paintbrush and then move it around to cover the cookie. Paint details into the wet icing using a smaller round-tip paintbrush. Sprinkle the colored sugar crystals and other toppings directly onto the wet icing. (For more details, see How to Apply Icing and Sprinkles, page 136.)

Stand back and let the kids go wild. The only help they'll need from you is to pass them a color they can't reach across the table, or to pull up a sleeve that has slipped.

The icing will dry and harden on its own in 10 minutes to 3 hours, depending on the humidity in the air and how thickly the icing is applied. Children are often impatient for results. To quick-dry the icing, place the finished cookies on a sheet tray in a 150-degree F oven until the surface hardens.

If there are kids leaving to go home when the cookie-decorating session is over, have little bags on hand with each child's name, so they can transport their handmade edible party favors.

Acknowledgments

During the time this book was written, I got engaged, married, and moved from my one-bedroom apartment on Manhattan's Upper West Side to a hand-built home in the hills of western Massachusetts.

It was difficult at times to keep my feet on the ground and my hands in the dough. In addition, most of these recipes were developed in the dog days of summer—the hottest, stickiest summer on record in the Northeast. Like a fisherman who watches the weather and waits for a good day to go out, I had to pick and choose my baking days.

Throughout these exciting distractions and meteorological obstacles, Bill Leßlond, my editor at Chronicle Books, was a voice of calm and reason. The bright idea for this book was his to begin with.

Permission to use the Got Milk?® slogan was granted by Jeff Manning, executive director of the California Milk Processor Board. He gave us his blessing as well as his support.

Tina Ujlaki, senior food editor at **Food & Wine**, made the match between Bill and me. Over the years that I've contributed to the magazine, Tina has been a steady light, an excellent editor, and a warm friend. The entire staff at **Food & Wine** has always been generous, supportive, and fun to work with. Test kitchen supervisor Marcia Kiesel is a baking buddy, travel companion, and an inspiration. A special thanks to those who have moved on, including Pamela Mitchell and Diana Sturgis.

The women in my early life instilled in me a love of baking: my mother, Betsie Cullen; my grandmother Frieda Kitzes; Geitel Gross; Anna Givner; Sydell Press; Leta Baron; and Joyce Packer.

A special thanks to Susie Mariano and Danny Lapidus, who rescued my manuscript at the eleventh hour, when my hard drive crashed, corrupting the disk. They accomplished what everyone said couldn't be done.

Along with my mother, my father, Gilbert Cullen, is a continual source of love, support, and sound advice. Michael Cullen, my brother and first baking buddy, endured my childhood "taste tests" and went on to create poetry out of it.

Diana Ulman, Margie Johnson, Sherry Chalfant Wolff, Jnani Chapman, Patty Burnstein, and Carlene Laughlin blur the line between family and friends. We've been laughing, crying, and baking together for longer than I can remember.

The hardest thing about leaving New York was leaving behind the girls in the 'hood—Penelope Pate-Green and Peggy Gibbons. Penel is a baking-mom extraordinare. Peggy G. is the other me. Many of my cookies are baked with the phone on my shoulder and her voice in my ear.

Profound thanks to Raychel Wade, who changed my life immeasurably, and to the parents who raised her.

To Marc Bregman, my dream man.

And to Andy Matlow, the man of my dreams.

Index

Table of Equivalents

NOTE: The exact equivalents in the following tables have been rounded for convenience.

Liquid and Dry Measures

U.S.	Metric
1/4 teaspoon	1.25 milliliters
1/2 teaspoon	2.5 milliliters
1 teaspoon	5 milliliters
1 tablespoon (3 teaspoons)	15 milliliters
1 fluid ounce (2 tablespoons)	30 milliliters
1/4 cup (4 tablespoons)	60 milliliters
1/3 cup	80 milliliters
1 cup (16 tablespoons)	240 milliliters
1 pint (2 cups)	480 milliliters
1 quart (4 cups, 32 ounces)	960 milliliters
1 gallon (4 quarts)	3.84 liters

(by weight)

U.S.	Metric
1 ounce	28 grams
1 pound	454 grams
2.2 pounds	1 kilogram

Length Measures

U.S.	Metric
1/8 inch	3 millimeters
1/4 inch	6 millimeters
1/2 inch	12 millimeters
1 inch	2.5 centimeters

Oven Temperatures

Fahrenheit	Celsius	Gas
250	120	1/2
275	140	1
300	150	2
325	160	3
350	180	4
375	190	5
400	200	6
425	220	7
450	230	8
475	240	9
500	260	10